CELEBRATING THE SIUSLAW: A CENTURY OF GROWTH

WARD TONSFELDT, Ph.D

TABLE OF CONTENTS

Finishing the Century

INTRODUCTION

INTRODUCTION AND A NOTE ON SOURCES

This history celebrates 100 years of the Siuslaw National Forest—1908 to 2008. The intent has been to feature the voices of the people who worked on the Forest and lived in the surrounding communities. We are fortunate to have a very rich collection of documents, photos, and interviews to tell the story of the Siuslaw. Forest Archaeologist Phyllis Steeves has done a remarkable job of collecting and curating these materials in her 20-year tenure on the Forest.

Among the documents are the memoirs and photographs of Corydon P. Cronk, who worked on the Siuslaw from 1910 to 1911 as an Assistant Ranger on the Hebo District. Cronk's photographic skills and his droll narrative style bring his short time on the Forest to life. A few years later, in 1917, the U.S. entered World War I. The Sitka spruce on the Forest and throughout the coast country was deemed crucial for the war effort, and we have excellent records of this period in photos of William Prentiss and Army Signal Corps. We also have the records of the Spruce Production Division.

In 1919, the Forest finalized the comprehensive Lands Classification Atlas, documenting all the land within the Forest boundaries, in its bewildering complexity and diversity. A few years later, Region 6 began publishing the newsletter *Six Twenty-Six* with excellent coverage of events and personalities on the Siuslaw written by the participants. During the Depression, documents of New Deal agencies active on the Forest, like the Civilian Conservation Corps and the Resettlement Administration, add to the mix of viewpoints.

In 1941 Forest Supervisor Dahl J. Kirkpatrick (1939-1942) circulated a densely-written typescript, "A History of the Siuslaw National Forest, Oregon, as of December 31, 1939." This history was apparently prepared in response to a directive from the Regional Office in 1940 asking that each Region 6 forest prepare a history documenting their early years. Whether Kirkpatrick wrote the unsigned "History" is not entirely clear, but it provides an excellent view of the inner workings of decision-making on the Forest, especially during the turbulent 1930s. Beginning in 1940 and continuing through the 1980s, the Forest Supervisor's office prepared annual "History Notes" recording events and personalities on the Forest.

In addition to documents prepared under official auspices, there are memoirs prepared by retired Forest staff. Noteworthy among these are memoirs by Clarence W. Jacobs chronicling his work on the Forest from the 1950s through the 1980s, and District Ranger Edward S. Kerby's lively account of the World War II years.

The oral history program on the Siuslaw is very active. Book-length interviews of District Ranger F. James Lyne and Forest Supervisor Rex Wakefield (1952-1962) are especially useful. The ongoing oral history program has prepared collections of interviews with Heceta Head staff, thirty-year employees of the Forest, conscientious objectors from Camp Waldport, and Civilian Conservation Corps enrollees. These preserve the insight and background of participants in recent history. More conventional historical information is available in the excellent materials prepared for the Forest during the 1980s by Stephen Dow Beckham and by Stephanie Finucane.

The few published histories cited will be familiar to anyone who enjoys reading about the coast country. Several works published by the Lincoln County Historical Society deserve special notice. These are *Steam Toward the Sunset* by Lloyd Palmer and *The Land That Kept Its Promise* by Marjorie Hays. Twenty years ago, the Lincoln County Historical Society brought out a re-print of a remarkable publication from 1924 entitled *Pacific Spruce Corporation and its Subsidiaries.* This piece of corporate promotion prepared by B.A. Johnson and Archibald Whisnat provides amazing detail and photos of 1920s logging on Lincoln County lands that would later come into the Forest.

I have spoken with many people about this project in the last few months, and I appreciate their help. Forest Archaeologist Phyllis Steeves and Lloyd Palmer, historian and retired Siuslaw staff member, have added their knowledge and insight on countless occasions. I would also like to thank the Confederated Tribes of Siletz Indians and the Confederated Tribes of Coos, Lower Umpqua, and Siuslaw Indians for their help with Chapter 1.

Individuals who contributed their time and expertise include the following: Loyd Collett, Don Large, Ken McCall, Rich Babcock, Bruce Buckley, Joni Quarnstrom, Mike Harvey, Bruce Gainer, Frank Davis, Cindy McLain, George Buckingham, and Dick Spray.

Book design and layout by Jessi Rawlings

CHAPTER ONE

ORIGINS

NATIVE AMERICANS ON THE CENTRAL OREGON COAST

The land that is now the Siuslaw National Forest has a rich history reaching back thousands of years to the first people on the North American continent. The people who were there at the time of initial contact with Euro-Americans were groups of Native Americans living along the coast and maintaining patterns of life suited to the coastal environment. What we know of these people comes from languages and cultural traditions kept alive by tribal members, by Euro-Americans who recorded what they saw during the contact period, by the records of early ethnographers, and by data from archaeological investigations.

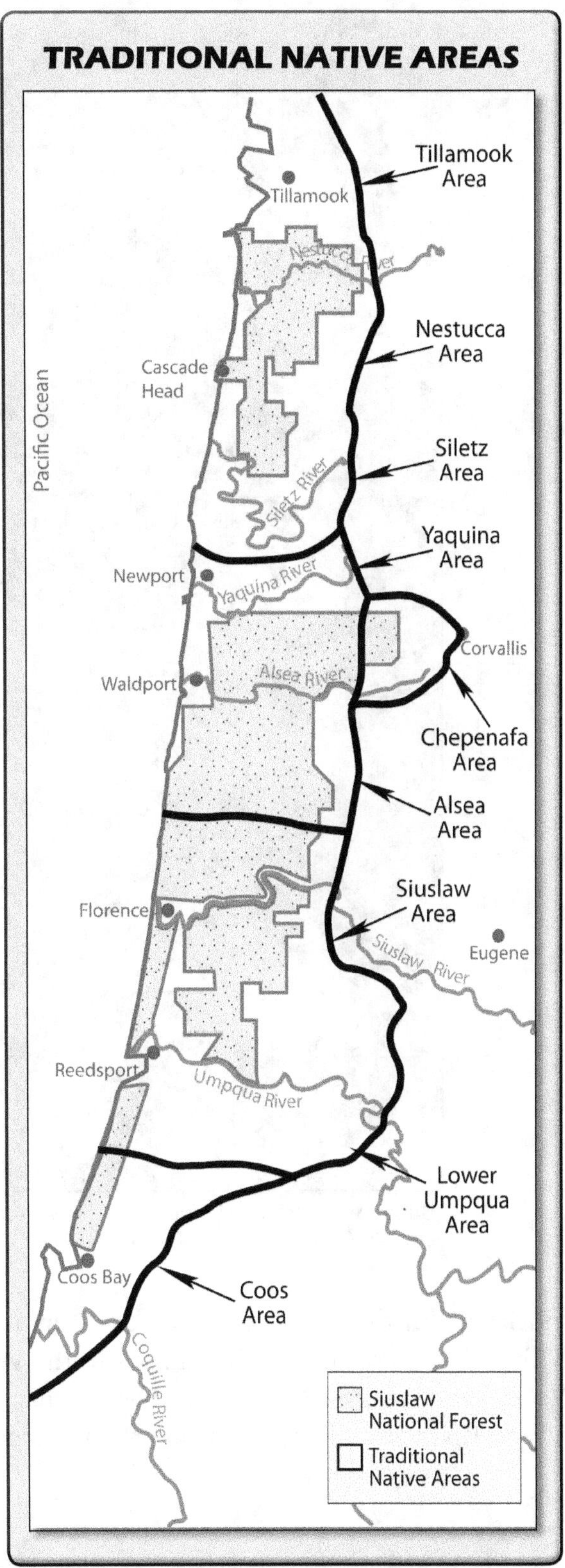

The indigenous peoples living on what is now the Siuslaw consisted of five groups differentiated by their languages and cultures. The people living on the coast when Euro-Americans first came into the country consisted of four groups ranging from the Tillamooks in the north to the Coos in the south. Further east, over the Coast Range crest, a group of Kalapuya speakers lived in the Marys River valley.

In the northern part of the central coast, from Tillamook Bay to the Yaquina River, were the Tillamook speakers, who were divided into two sub-groups by their dialects—the Tillamooks and the Siletz. To the south of the Tillamook speakers lived the Alsean speakers, who were also divided into two groups, the Yaquinans and the Alseans. South of the Alsea River, people living in the Siuslaw and Lower Umpqua River areas spoke

Basket weavers, Mary Young and her mother Molly Catfish.
Lincoln County Historical Society (LCHS) Collection.

Siuslawn. Further south, on Coos Bay were the Hanis and Miluk Coosan speakers. The Indians in the Willamette Valley spoke dialects of the Kalapuya language. In the Marys River area, the Chepenafa group predominated.

Bone points for fish harpoons.

The Tillamooks lived in favorable areas from Tillamook Head to Otter Rock, including Nehalem Bay, Tillamook Bay, Netarts Bay, the Nestucca estuary, the Salmon River, and the Siletz River. Like other Salish peoples, they built substantial wooden canoes which they used in the bays and ocean for fishing and sea-mammal hunting. Woodworking technology extended to their houses, which were built from cedar planks. They were also sophisticated with fibers, making baskets, weirs, and fishing lines from various plant fibers. U.S. Superintendent of Indian Affairs Joel Palmer estimated in 1854 the population for the Tillamook groups at around 200 total, divided into six bands.[1] Population figures from the 1800s do not represent the historic norms, since diseases spread after contact with Europeans substantially reduced native populations.

Coast Indians built houses of split cedar planks, such as this one on the lower Umpqua River, ca. 1857-1858. OHS photo.

The Tillamooks' neighbors to the south, the Yaquinas and Alseas, were also reduced by imported diseases, especially smallpox and tuberculosis. The language of the Alseas was similar to people living to the south, but they shared elements of material culture with northern coastal peoples. The Alseas also benefited from the sophisticated coastal trade network.

South of the Alsea speakers, the Siuslawn and Lower Umpqua speakers lived on the Siuslaw, Smith, and lower Umpqua rivers. The Coos had a distinct language that was itself divided into two dialects, both spoken on Coos Bay. The Siuslaw, Lower Umpqua, and Coos are now affiliated through a confederation of these tribes. This affiliation grew out of their experiences on the Coast Indian Reservation after 1855 and their common legal struggle with the government for land and compensation. The original territory of these groups extended north as far as Tenmile Creek (Lane County) and south to the southwest shoreline of Coos Bay. To the east, their territory extended over the Coast Range crest into the Willamette Valley.

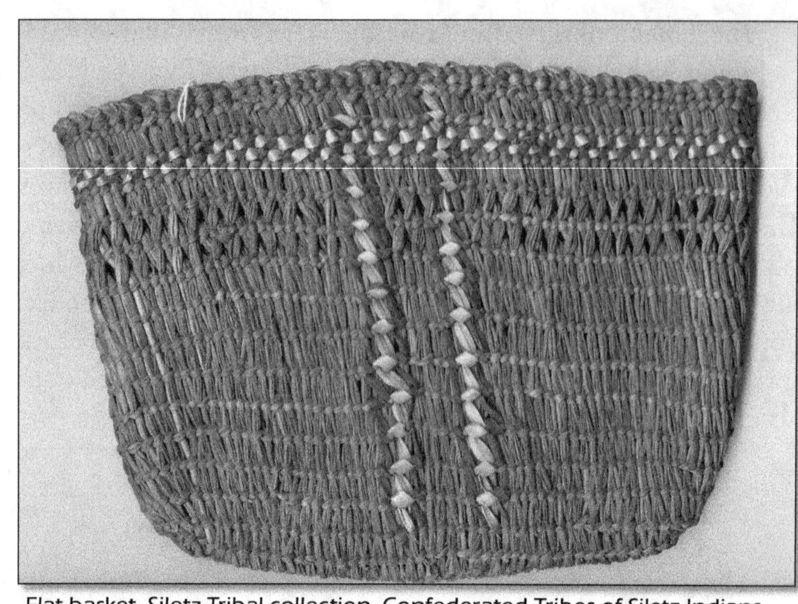

Flat basket, Siletz Tribal collection, Confederated Tribes of Siletz Indians.

The Siuslaws, Lower Umpquas, and Coos lived on fish and large game animals which could be preserved by smoking and drying. They caught salmon, steelhead, lamprey, smelt, and sturgeon in the rivers and bays. Mollusks and crabs were available in the bays and on the beaches. Plant foods included camas, fern root, various berries, and acorns from the Willamette Valley.[2] Elk, deer, and sea mammals were among the large animals regularly hunted. Beached whales were an important source of oil.

Bone fish hooks and nettle fiber line.

The technology of these three groups included woodworking to produce plank houses and canoes which could exceed 20 feet in length. These canoes were capable of going to sea as needed for hunting and fishing. Coos informants at the turn of the century provided a list of ten different structure types built from cedar planks. The planks were used for fencing as well. Nineteenth century visitors observed that the plank houses were built over an excavated area, framed with poles, and sided with tied-on planking. The roofs were gables covered with overlapping planks. Within the houses would be fireplaces, sleeping platforms, and storage areas. The material culture included items made from stone, wood, bone, antler, and a variety of plant fibers. Spruce roots, iris leaf fibers, tules, cedar bark, and sea grass provided fibers for clothing, mats, baskets, fishing lines, weirs, and nets.

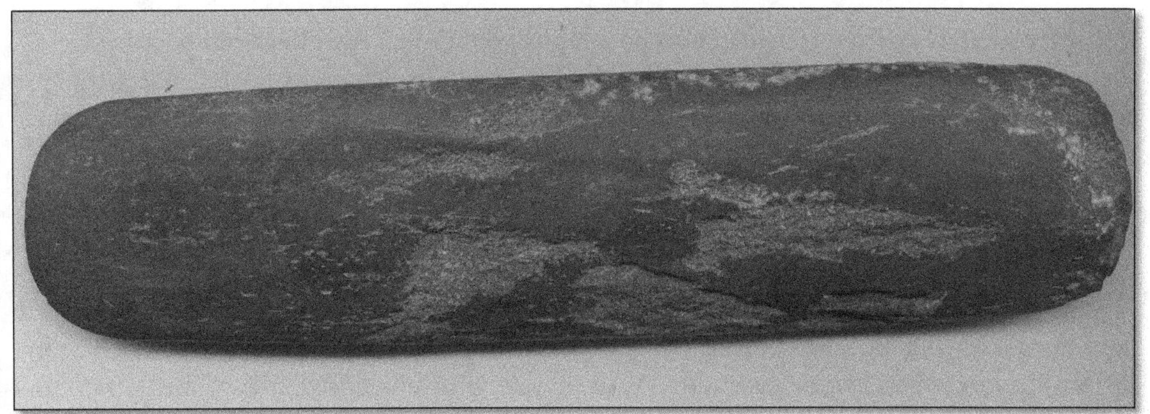

Wedge for splitting cedar, made from nephrite, traded from the north.

East of the Coast Range, groups of Kalapuya occupied the valley of the Willamette River and its tributaries. Beginning with the area east of Tillamook Bay, these were the Yamhill, the Luckiamute, and the Chepenafa, who lived on the Marys River. By 1900, the Yamhills numbered 30, the Luckiamutes 28, and the Chepenafa 25.[3] The Kalapuya came into contact with Europeans and Metis from the Hudson's Bay Company at Fort Vancouver much earlier than the coastal groups. They had access to ferrous metal trade goods, ceramic items, and perhaps horses. Beginning with the Euro-American settlement of the Willamette Valley in the 1840s, they were displaced from their homes as the valley "settled up."

CONTACT, TREATIES, AND THE RESERVATION

There are few written records or archaeological data of contact between people of the coast and Europeans or Asians before the European explorations in the sixteenth and seventeenth centuries. The Tillamook oral tradition of a foreign vessel landing (or wrecking) near Nehalem Bay is generally thought to refer to a Spanish ship from Manila because these vessels made landfall somewhere on the Northwest coast on their annual voyage from Manila to Acapulco. There is also a persistent controversy surrounding the voyage of Elizabethan mariner Sir Francis Drake. Drake sailed north up the coast of North America and possibly landed on the Oregon coast. In more recent years, there have been a few instances of vessels from Asia crossing the Pacific to the coast of Oregon or Washington when lost or disabled. With these exceptions noted, it is probably safe to say that the Indians of the coast lived without much foreign contact until the end of the eighteenth century.

At that time—in 1776—British explorer Captain James Cook sailed along the central Oregon coast mapping and naming prominent landmarks including Cape Arago, Cape Foulweather, and Cape Perpetua. After Cook, there was lively competition between British, Spanish, French, Russians, and Americans for trade along the coast. American mariner Robert Gray made contact with the coastal peoples in 1788, visiting Tillamook Bay and entering the Columbia River on a later voyage in 1792. The Lewis and Clark expedition wintered at the mouth of the Columbia in 1805-1806, and the trading post of Astoria was established in 1810. The presence of foreigners on the coast led to the terrible epidemics that ravaged native peoples in the early nineteenth century.

Annie Di Tallo, 1909. LCHS photo.

By 1848, the coastal people had a new challenge.[4] Miners entering the Rogue River drainage came into conflict with the tribes of the Rogue River and Upper Umpqua. Hostilities began in 1851 and continued until the end of 1855. The continuing conflict in southwestern Oregon made the Euro-American settlers as far away as the Willamette Valley nervous, and there was political pressure for the government to pacify the tribes. During the spring and summer, the remaining Rogue and Upper Umpqua peoples were removed to a reservation established at Grand Ronde on the Yamhill River. The Kalapuya in the Willamette Valley—including those in Marys River area—were removed to Grand Ronde at this time as well. Although this reservation was in use as early as 1856, it was not officially established until June of 1857.

In the meantime, the tribes of the central coast—the Tillamooks, Alseas, Siuslaws, Coos, and Lower Umpquas—were generally tolerant of the Euro-Americans. Euro-Americans had begun settlements on the lower Umpqua River and on Tillamook Bay in the early 1850s, but the Indians got along with their new neighbors. Joel Palmer contacted the central coast groups in 1855 to negotiate a treaty. As a result, the Coast Indian Reservation was created in November of 1855.

The new reservation, exceeding one million acres, extended from Cape Lookout south to the Siltcoos River, and extended inland to the Coast Range crest. This encompassed some of the traditional lands of the Tillamooks, most of the traditional lands of the Yaquinas and Alseas, some of the lands of the Siuslaws, but little of the traditional territory of the Lower Umpquas or Coos. Beginning in 1856, the government moved 26 bands of people from western Oregon, northern California, and southwestern Washington onto the new reservation. The Lower Umpquas, Coos, and several groups from the south-central coast were moved forcibly to the U.S. Army's Fort Umpqua in the spring and summer of 1856. The Indian Service established an agency on the Siletz River at Siletz, and later the Alsea sub-agency at Yachats.

The agency at Siletz and the sub-agency at Yachats became centers of the reservation. Total numbers of Indians in the northern portion of the reservation was about 2,000 in 1856; 300 lived

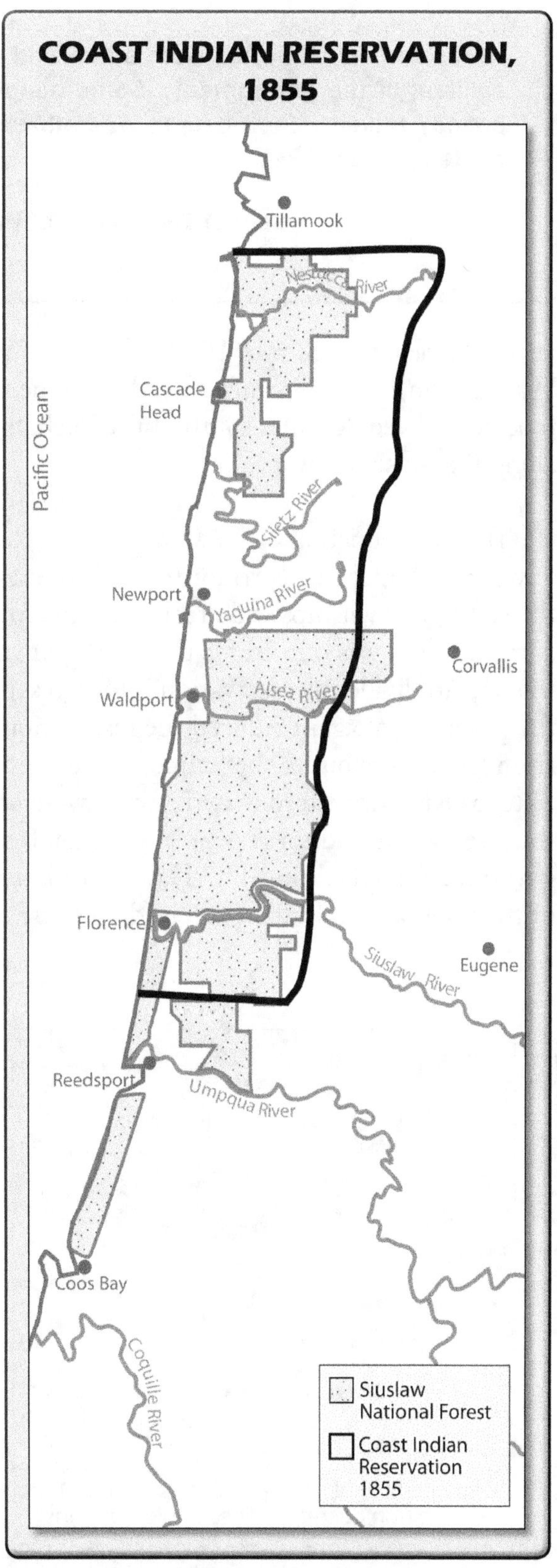

It was summer time, we were all herded down to the ocean at Port Orford by the soldiers of the government. Some people were crying, others were just quiet—nobody talked. Each person was allowed only one package or pack, generally made up in a basket.

George Thompson, of the Coquilles, quoted in Marjorie H. Hays, *The Land That Kept its Promise*

at the Alsea sub-agency in 1872.[5] These numbers reflect the 26 groups from Oregon, Washington, and California moved onto the Coast Indian Reservation. The Siuslaws reportedly lived 30 miles south of the Yachats sub-agency at their traditional locations along the Siuslaw River

The first reduction of the Coast Indian Reservation came in 1865 when the government opened a corridor through the reservation from the Coast Range crest to the sea, four townships wide from Yaquina Head to the mouth of the Alsea River. No compensation was offered for this taking of valuable and useful land. The effect of this was to divide the reservation into two separate halves. After ten years, in 1875, the government again reduced the reservation. The northern part of the reservation from Cape Lookout to the Salmon River, and the southern part from Alsea Bay to the Siltcoos River were terminated. There were at least 300 Indians living on this part of the reservation, and these people were displaced from their homes.[6] Finally, in 1892, the government applied the 1887 Dawes or General Allotment Act to the remaining part of the reservation. Indians received 160 acre allotments, and the remainder of the Coast

Government Hill, Siletz Agency, 1910. Tribal Archives, Confederated Tribes of Siletz Indians.

In 1872, the Indians at the Yachats Agency lived in about ten board houses, 16 feet by 20 feet or 8 feet by 12 feet. There were cattle sheds, a blacksmith shop, and buildings to house the farm implements. The fields were divided into seven parcels for convenience of seeding. All told, there were 35 acres of oats, 20 of potatoes, and 14 of wheat and some timothy and general garden of mostly carrots and turnips.

Marjorie H. Hays, *The Land That Kept its Promise*

Five generations of Siletz women, Molly Carmichaels, Jane Yanna, Maimie Strong, Molly Catfish. LCHS photo.

Julie Meggison. LCHS photo.

John and Lily Ponsee, Nettie West. LCHS photo.

As a general rule these are industrious [people] and try to make a living for themselves; they no longer live in groups as separate tribes but have nearly all of them, or at least the heads of families, taken their land as surveyed, have built houses on the same and are making, some more, some less, use of the ground... some of their houses would lose nothing by comparison with many of the whites. As a general rule, they go decently dressed.

David Fagan, *History of Benton County, Oregon*, 1885

Indian Reservation passed into the public domain. For the 191,798 unallotted acres, the tribes were paid $142,600.

The actions of the government in 1892 are difficult to understand, let alone justify. The Dawes Act was the law of the land after 1888, but it was applied inconsistently. Large reservations across the country were able to keep unallotted lands as tribal trust

Chantell Indian allotment homestead near Logsden, after 1900. Tribal Archives, Confederated Tribes of Siletz Indians.

lands after individual allotments had been made. In Oregon, the Klamath and Warm Spring reservations kept unallotted lands as range and timber lands for the benefit of the tribes. The Klamaths held 863,815 unallotted acres and the Warm Springs held 321,915 unallotted acres after the individual allotments had been made. In Washington, the Yakamas retained 422,444 unallotted acres, and the Colvilles retained 220,000.[7]

> **On October 31, 1892, a treaty agreement was entered into, according to the official records, between Reuben P. Boise, William H. Odell (he of the Oregon State School land notoriety) and H.H. Harding, commissioners on the part of the U.S., and the chiefs headmen and other male adults of the Alsea and other kindred tribes residing on the Coast Indian Reservation, whereby the Indians disposed of all their holdings, aggregating ten full townships in extent and embracing some of the finest timber in the world, for the paltry sum of $142,000! What the Indians were coaxed into giving for this relatively insignificant amount represents an area equivalent to about 1,300 homestead claims of 160 acres each, or practically 200,000 acres in round numbers and is worth today [1907] at a conservative estimate more than $8,000,000. If Uncle Sam could do as well on all his real estate investments, he could afford to retire, satisfied with his sagacity, if not his conscience.**
>
> **Stephen A.D. Puter, *Looters of the Public Domain***

EURO-AMERICAN EXPANSION AND THE CENTRAL OREGON COAST

The nineteenth century migration of Americans, Europeans, and Asians into the western portion of the United States and Canada is one of the distinctive events of recent world history. The western frontier of North America captured the world's imagination at the time, and it has become a permanent part of American cultural identity. Crossing the Great Plains, gold mining in California and the Rocky Mountains, and cattle ranching in the Great Basin were celebrated in the literature of the times and in much popular culture that has followed.

There were, however, some areas of the west where Euro-Americans arrived late in the settlement period. For most of the nineteenth century, the central coast of Oregon remained one of these regions, although reasonably close to population centers further inland. Land transportation within the Coast Range was difficult, and the lack of decent harbors made coastal navigation chancy, except at a few favored places. As a result, it attracted few Euro-American immigrants through the middle of the nineteenth century.

The coast offered immigrants an excellent opportunity for survival but a poor outlook for prosperity. The weather was mild; fresh water was plentiful; fish and game abounded. Even the most improvident new-comers could feed themselves. The resources of the coast were difficult to turn into cash, however. The mild climate and ample rain invited

Euro-American settlement on the central Oregon coast occurred in five phases:

A) Ongoing settlement from the 1850s north of Lookout Point, south of the Siltcoos River and east of the Coast Range summit. Settlement between these landmarks closed after the Coast Indian Reservation was formed in 1855

B) Settlement on Coast Indian Reservation lands after 1865 when the east-west corridor through the reservation between Yaquina Head and the mouth of the Alsea was opened

C) Settlement on Coast Indian Reservation lands after 1875 when the reservation south of the Alsea and north of the Salmon River was terminated

D) Settlement on Coast Indian Reservation lands after 1892 when the remainder of the reservation was terminated by the effects of the Dawes Act

E) Settlement on Siuslaw National Forest lands after 1908 as a result of the Forest Homestead Act of 1906

farming, but the narrow river valleys did not produce a high surplus of products. Stock raising was possible in the open areas, but there were few of these available. Dairying was an option in the Tillamook Bay area. Goats did well throughout the coast, but the market for mohair was not reliable.

The impressive stands of timber were worthless without sawmills to manufacture lumber and ships or railroads to bring the lumber to market. Salmon required canning or salting and a means of transportation. Oysters offered some hope for commerce, but the intertidal beds were soon exhausted. The financial mainstay of most settlers was cascara bark—also called "chittum"—which was easy to harvest and process, and brought a price as high as 20 cents per pound.

The pattern of settlement that emerged in isolated valleys of the Coast Range was subsistence farming. Settlers cleared enough land to provide an area for a garden, berry patch, orchard, and pasturage for a few cattle, sheep, or goats. Settlers supplemented the

> **Were it not for the large amount of Chittum bark in these mountains, it would have been almost impossible for these settlers to have made a living.**
>
> **Siuslaw National Forest Supervisor Anson E. Cohoon, 1912**

production of their "place" by hunting and fishing, especially for the salmon that crowded the streams in the spring and fall. Cash was available by selling cascara bark or working for wages in logging, fishing, or construction. If a homestead had timber, that could be sold to a lumber company.

This pattern of life was comfortable enough and persisted until the Great Depression. At that time, sources of cash dwindled. Settlers with good titles to their homesteads could mortgage them, or they could stop paying local property tax, which was the major cash outlay for many families. But neither of these strategies worked well. Mortgages required additional cash to service them, and withholding property taxes led to county tax liens. In the later years of the Depression, the Resettlement Administration bought up old homesteads that were abandoned, logged off, or tax-delinquent. The Depression, Resettlement, and World War II conscription ended a way of life that had persisted in the Coast Range since the 1860s.

MEANS OF ACQUIRING LAND

Individuals seeking land on the coast for their own use had several options as public land programs developed through the nineteenth century.

OREGON DONATION CLAIMS (1850) Men who had cultivated public domain lands for four years prior to 1850 could obtain title to 320 acres; their wives could obtain an additional 320. Immigrants claiming land after 1850 but before 1855 could claim 160 acres and wives could claim an additional 160.

HOMESTEAD CLAIMS (1862) Citizens or people intending to become citizens who were heads of households, single men, or widows could buy 160 acres or 80 acres in the public domain for $1.25 per acre or $2.50 per acre respectively. Settlers could claim 160 acres and obtain title without purchase by meeting settlement requirements. "Commutated" homesteads could be purchased at $1.25 per acre any time after six months of filing. Legislation in 1904 and 1909 enlarged the size of new the claims to 320 acres in the nine Western states.

TIMBER AND STONE ACT CLAIMS (1878, 1892) Citizens could claim 160 acres of timber land "not fit for agriculture" and pay $2.50 per acre for title.

DAWES ACT ALLOTMENTS (1887) Tribal members on the Coast Indian Reservation could claim 160 acres on the reservation for personal use. Normally, the government held these allotments in trust for 25 years, then issued title. However, the Act of May 27, 1902, allowed heirs of tribal members to sell inherited allotments. Further, the Burke Act of May 6, 1906, authorized the Secretary of the Interior to issue title to allottees who demonstrated "competence and capability" in managing their own affairs. Under the terms of the 1902 and 1906 legislation, then, tribal members could sell allotments on the secondary market without waiting for the 25 trust period to expire.

FOREST HOMESTEAD CLAIMS (1906) Citizens could claim 160 acres within the Siuslaw National Forest (after 1908) if the lands were "best suited" for agriculture. The Siuslaw was officially open to Forest Homestead settlement after 1908, then closed, then opened again from 1913 to 1916.

SETTLEMENT ON THE CENTRAL OREGON COAST BEFORE 1855

The land now within the Siuslaw National Forest was largely contained within the Coast Indian Reservation between 1855 and 1892. The exceptions are the Dallas city watershed, Marys Peak, and the lands south of Siltcoos River, which was the southern boundary of the reservation. Siuslaw National Forest lands in this southern area include the following: the Umpqua River mouth, lands between the Smith River and the Umpqua River, the dunes south of Winchester Bay, and the Coos Bay north spit. Lands that are now in the Elliott State Forest were originally part of the Siuslaw National Forest, but were all located south of the Siltcoos River and were not in the Coast Indian Reservation.

During the early 1850s, Euro-American settlement on the central coast was concentrated at Tillamook Bay to the north and the Umpqua River and Coos Bay to the south. In 1850, after the Donation Claims were available, a group in California organized as Winchester, Paine, and Co. to explore the south-central Oregon coast and promote settlement. They sailed into the estuary of the Umpqua River and platted ten town sites including Umpqua City, Scottsburg, Elkton, and Winchester. Immigrants settled in the Umpqua estuary during the 1850s. South of the Umpqua at Coos Bay, settlement followed the wreck of the steamer *Captain Lincoln* in 1852. Passengers stranded in Coos Bay included a number of single men and three families who subsequently settled there.[8]

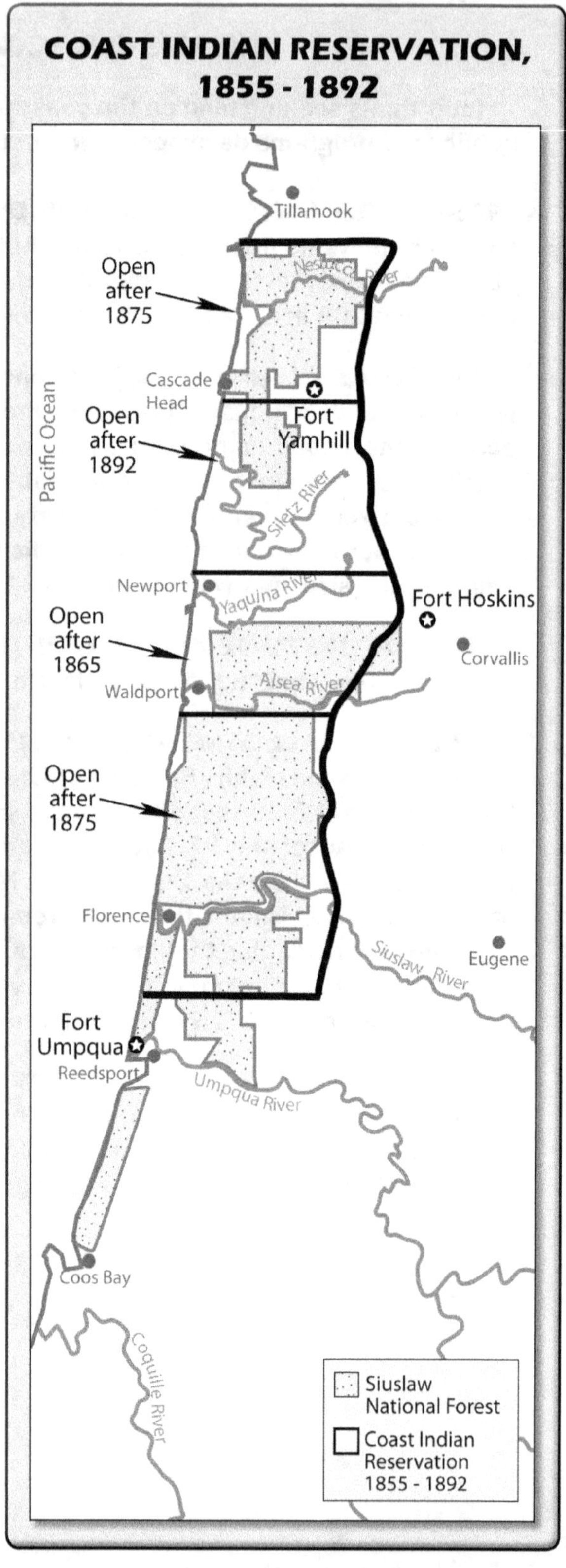

Meanwhile, on the north central Oregon coast, a group sailed from the Columbia River to Tillamook Bay in 1850. Joseph Champion, the only member of the group who persevered through the first dismal winter, camped in a hollow spruce tree. Other settlers joined the colony in sufficient numbers to form their own county by 1853.[9] By 1855 the Tillamook settlers were able to build a small vessel, the schooner *Morning Star*, which established regular communication with the outside world.

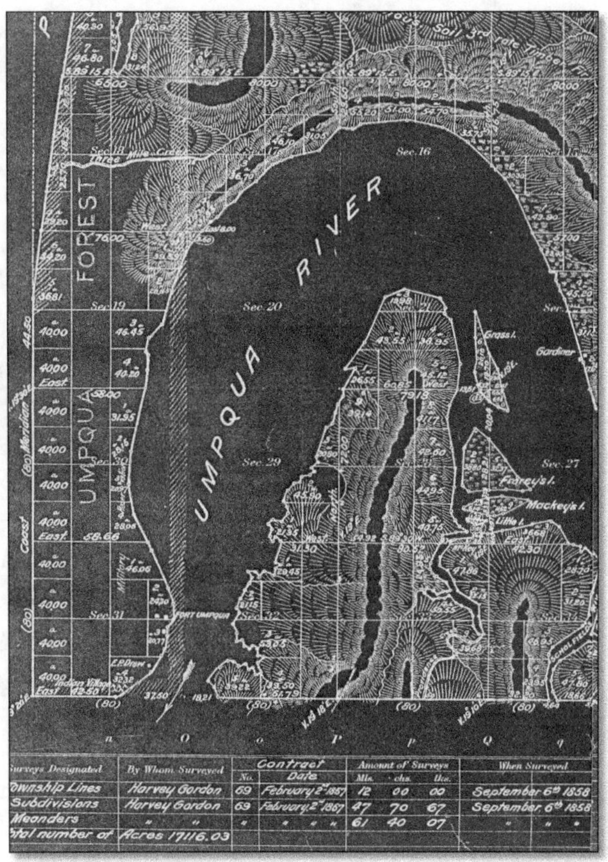

General Land Office map showing Fort Umpqua and Gardiner, ca. 1858.

By 1853, then, Euro-American population centers on the central Oregon coast were established in the Umpqua/Coos Bay area on the south, and on Tillamook Bay on the north. These were relatively robust. In choosing the land between the Umpqua and Tillamook Bay for the Coast Indian Reservation, Joel Palmer was acknowledging the status quo. Euro-Americans were established in navigable bays north and south of the reservation, but the coast between these two points had little Euro-American settlement. After 1856, federal troops were stationed at Fort Umpqua to the south, Fort Hoskins to the east, and Fort Yamhill to the north to keep Euro-Americans out of the reservation and Indians in.

Head of navigation on the Umpqua River, Scottsburg, ca. 1915.

In December of 1865, President Andrew Johnson signed an executive order opening a corridor four townships wide through the Coast Indian Reservation from the Coast Range crest to the Pacific. The avowed purpose was to open a transportation route from the Willamette Valley to the Pacific, but observers noted that it precipitated a land rush as settlers and speculators applied for land through the 1862 homestead program.[10]

When land was officially available in the corridor in January, 1866, four soldiers from Fort Hoskins were among the first to file claims. The soldiers brought saw-mill machinery from San Francisco to their claims on Depot Slough and built the first mill in the area. A fifth former soldier, Samuel Case, built a lodging house, which he named "Ocean House," and began a community, which he named Newport. Oyster merchants Winant and Company built a store and supplied it by ship from San Francisco. By July of 1866, six months after the first legal settlement, the *Corvallis Gazette* estimated that there were 300 new residents in the bay.[11] Newport was touted as the future "San Francisco of Oregon."[12]

In 1866 the toll road of the Corvallis and Aquina Bay Military Wagon Road Company was opened from Corvallis to Newport. This road provided reasonable access from the Willamette Valley to Newport, and also opened up the inland valleys along its route. These areas further inland also attracted settlers. For example, the upper drainage of Big Elk Creek, a tributary of the Yaquina River, appealed to the Grant family and other settlers in the early 1870s.[13]

The pattern of development on Yaquina Bay reflected tourism, trade, and a certain urbanity from the beginning. Twelve miles to the south, Alsea Bay also got settlers in 1866, but the pace was slower. Settlers arrived on Alsea Bay in 1865 and claimed lands at the head of the bay. The first school was operating by 1871.[14] Unlike Newport, Waldport was founded after the first settlement period was over in 1884. In her lively account of the settlement of south Lincoln County, Marjorie H. Hays noted that her grandfather came into the Alsea Bay country in 1886 but found all the attractive land on the bay and on the ocean already taken. Nevertheless, the land further up the river was well worth the work of homesteading.

Access to the upper Alsea Valley was delayed by the lack of a road over the mountains to the Willamette Valley. No adequate road was available until 1919, when one was built as part of the Forest Roads Program, combining federal, state, and county funds amounting to $367,000 for construction.[15]

> **You spoke of land for sale here. Well, there is a nice place on the river about four miles below here—160 acres with bottom land a good orchard; house, barn, hay meadow; nice fountain (spring) nearby. It is five miles from Waldport, which is at the mouth of the Alsea River. They are one miles from school and there will be a road—there is a horse trail now. Most of the travel is by water.**
>
> **Martha French, October 5, 1887 (in Hays, *The Land That Kept its Promise*)**

SETTLEMENT AFTER 1875

Termination of the northern portion of the reservation from Cape Lookout to the Salmon River, and the southern portion from Alsea Bay to the Siltcoos River made roughly 1,200 square miles of reservation lands available to settlers and investors after 1875. The southern portion of the former reservation included the drainages of the Siuslaw River, the Yachats River, and several streams with direct access to the ocean. The northern portion included the drainage of the Nestucca and the Little Nestucca and the country around Mt. Hebo.

Early settlement in the lower Nestucca valley led to the establishment of the Oretown post office in 1877. Other communities formed after the northern reservation lands opened in 1875 include Dolph, Hebo, Meda, and Neskowin.[16] As with other areas of the central coast, the valley lands attracted immigrants, with the lower valleys and the coast itself exercising the strongest pull.

South of the Alsea River, the lands opened in 1875 offered some of the best opportunities for settlement and commerce on the central coast. Areas targeted included the lower Siuslaw Valley, the lands adjacent to the coastal lakes, and the North Fork of the Smith River. The first cannery was established on the Siuslaw estuary in 1876. Florence, Acme, and Glenada were established on the estuary; Mapleton was near the head of tidewater.

Settlement in this area continued through the 1880s and 1890s with land seekers arriving from the Willamette Valley, but also from other parts of the U.S. and Europe. The Oregon coast appealed to people from northern Europe, especially Germany, Finland, Norway, and Sweden. Marjorie H. Hays notes that her family came from northern Europe, stopped for a year in Minnesota, and then found the Alsea Valley. Settlers had difficulty getting established financially. Nearly all of the written accounts mention the resourceful ways the settlers found for getting cash.

Modest homestead on burned over land. C.P. Cronk photo, 1910-1911.

Self sustaining farm units could not be developed except in the most favorable spots. There was nothing which could be sold from the ranches. Settlers were obliged to go out at some time during the year and earn a grub stake...

A History of the Siuslaw National Forest, Oregon, as of December 31, 1939

Marjorie H. Hays reports that her family included skilled woodworkers who found employment that saw them through the most difficult times.

> *You might wonder what people did for a living in those hazardous times and so far from supplies. For three years Papa helped build the Heceta Light House, tediously and skillfully applying his old world techniques doing the interior work in the two keepers' houses, which boasted very impressive stairways... He helped Mr. Gwynn build a large house...copied after those around Dallas and Corvallis...Finally, working out and making oars and floats for Alsea fishermen he was able to buy a circular saw and mandrel to build his long dreamed-of sawmill.*
>
> Marjorie H. Hays, *The Land That Kept its Promise*

Other settlers relied on salmon fishing for cash if there was a cannery nearby, or for home use as salted fish.

> *It is the running season for salmon, and fishing takes precedence over everything else—the annual harvest of the winter grubstake.*
>
> Siuslaw National Forest Supervisor Clyde R. Seitz, 1907-1908

Cannery at Waldport.

Milk cows and other livestock were important to homestead families. C.P. Cronk photo, 1910-1911.

Trapping or hunting fur-bearing animals was another way to earn the much-needed cash.

> *Our cash income in the first years was from hunting and trapping. We hunted deer for their hides and meat. The red hides, which are thicker, taken in July and August, brought forty cents a pound. A good dry deer hide weighs about six pounds for which we got $2.40. The blue hides of winter brought twenty cents a pound. We also trapped mink, wildcat, and bear. Bear hides brought $8.00 to $10.00 and what is more, bear provided the major source of fat for frying, and in many homes it was used as a spread in place of butter.*

George P. Stonefield quoted in Bogue and Yunker, *Proved Up On Ten Mile Creek*

Home of prosperous settlers, Pacific City. C.P. Cronk photo, 1910-1911.

SETTLEMENT AFTER 1892

In 1892, Indians on the Coast Indian Reservation received 160 acre allotments. The lands left after the allotments were claimed amounted to 191,798 acres in what is now northern Lincoln County. The government paid the tribes $142,000 for these lands, and then opened them for homestead entry. Homesteaders filed on some of the new public domain lands, and timber investors acquired others. The allotments were to remain in trust for 25 years under the original Dawes Act legislation, but subsequent legislation in 1902 and 1906 enabled the allottees to receive title sooner.

Many tribal members filed allotments on the last portion of the original reservation, which lay between Yaquina Head and the Salmon River estuary. However, unclaimed public lands on other parts of the former reservation were also available for allotments. The banks of the Salmon River, the upper Siletz River, and the shore north of Cape Foulweather were popular for allotments and were good choices.[17] Similar patterns occurred in Lane and Douglas counties.

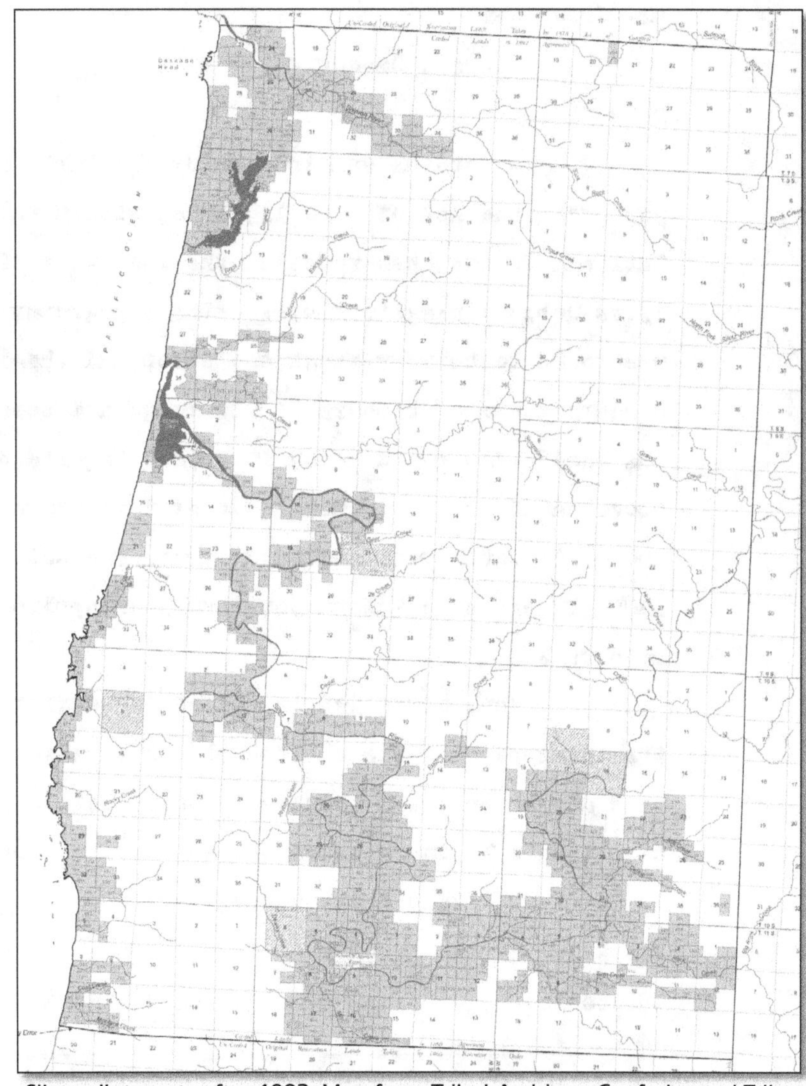

Siletz allotments after 1892. Map from Tribal Archives. Confederated Tribes of Siletz Indians.

The Forest Homestead Act of June 11, 1906 had a significant impact on the Siuslaw National Forest. The law reflected Westerners' concern that they would be deprived of good homestead lands that were included within the boundaries of national forests. Since the newly-formed Forest Service could not survey all the land within the national forests at once, a policy developed under which homesteaders claimed lands, and the Forest

L
Siuslaw-Settlement,
May, Jesse, #473.

Mr. Jesse May, October 7, 1914.

Fisher, Oregon.

Dear Sir:

A careful examination of the land applied for by you under the Act of June 11, 1906, within the Siuslaw National Forest, has revealed the fact that it is not chiefly valuable for agriculture. The topography of the area was found to be very rough and steep and the land supports a heavy stand of timber. The rough and steep character of the land alone would debar it from being listed under the above named act. Since lands of this character cannot be opened to settlement and entry under the Act of June 11, 1906, I regret to inform you that your application must be rejected.

Your attention is called to Regulation L-53 on the third page of the enclosed blank by which you will note that any appeal from this decision rejecting your application should be in accordance with certain instructions.

Very truly yours,

C. J. Buck.

Enclosure: Acting District Forester.

Letter from the Forest Service notifying homesteader that his claim has been denied.

Service determined whether they were suitable for agriculture after the fact. This policy invited abuse, and many forest homesteads were chosen for their timber value rather than their agricultural potential. C.P. Cronk, working on the Hebo Ranger District in 1910 noted that investigating "June 11" forest homestead claims was a major part of his work.

The Siuslaw was officially open to forest homestead claims when it became a national forest in 1908. Then it was closed to homesteading in 1910, re-opened in 1913, and finally closed permanently in 1916. The total number of forest homestead claims filed on the Siuslaw was 1,115.[18] As Cronk and virtually all other commentators point out, some claims were opportunistic and even fraudulent, but many were legitimate. The Forest Service was required to adjudicate forest homestead claims, and—not surprisingly—their decisions were not always well-received. Many of the forest homestead applicants were desperate, as the public land in the U.S. available for entry was rapidly diminishing after the turn of the century. They perceived the forest homestead program to be their last chance. The best lands were gone. Those that remained were not ideal homesteads, but had some potential.

Perhaps the greatest problem with the forest homestead program was the difficulties it created between the Forest Service and the public. Some disappointed homesteaders responded by incendiarism—deliberately setting forest fires to damage the forest and frustrate the Forest Service.

Old diaries revealed that a hot-bed of incendiary fire was a constant threat in the Niagara drainage during the '20s. During the late fall and early spring, an east wind prevailed and the fern fields were very dry.

District Ranger Rolfe Anderson, "Hebo District Historical Notes" 1966

Unscrupulous individuals took advantage of the confusion associated with the forest homestead program.

> *Lorenzo E. Doel... posed as an official land locator, had a badge proclaiming to all and sundry that he was an official land locator. He would charge $50 to locate suckers on government land that was not open to entry.*
>
> District Ranger Edward S. Kerby, 1945

IN REPLY PLEASE REFER TO "B" Mx 4 Portland 01149 – Pat 239993

14 Forester

FOREST SERVICE
JAN 4 1912
Referred to

4—080

DEPARTMENT OF THE INTERIOR

GENERAL LAND OFFICE

WASHINGTON

January 3, 19

ADDRESS ONLY THE COMMISSIONER OF THE GENERAL LAND OFFICE

FOREST SERVICE
District 6
RECEIVED
JAN 11 1912
Referred to
LANDS

FOREST SERVICE
District 6
RECEIVED
JAN 11 1912
Referred to
LANDS

The Forester,
Forest Service,
Washington,
D. C.

Sir:

In compliance with your request, you are informed that Portland No. 01149 Homestead Patent, No. 239993 in the name of James C. Huntsucker, for the S½ SW¼ SW¼ SE¼, lot 7, Sec 13, Tp. 12 S. R. 11 W. in the Siuslaw National Forest, issued Dec. 21, 1911.

Very respectfully,

Fred Dennett.

Commissioner.

Letter from the Forest Service notifying homesteader that his claim is approved.

Homestead children cutting firewood in snow. C.P. Cronk photo, 1910-1911.

Once a homesteader had filed and "located" on a parcel of land, removing the family could be quite difficult. All of their capital as well as a significant amount of labor was likely invested in the claim.

The Forest Service was sometimes asked to adjudicate cases where the ownership was far from clear.

Here [to Schooner Creek], for example, came Gustave Granfor, a bachelor, who put up a house and cleared three acres, became homesick, and returned to his native land [Finland], only to be killed in the revolution of 1917, previous to which he had mortgaged his place for $200 to Jack Wick, a storekeeper, who in turn passed it on to his successor in business, who lost it to a wholesale grocer, who sold it to a new settler, who lost it on a mortgage to a Portland bank, who sold it back to the U.S.

A History of the Siuslaw National Forest, Oregon, as of December 31, 1939

Homestead claims... varied from a real home on burned over fern patches to claims with over 100,000 board feet of old-growth timber per acre where there was no pretense to meet the homestead requirement. On the other hand there were in heavily timbered areas, claims where the homesteader hoped to get something for the timber, yet took the claim because he loved the surroundings and endeavored to conform to the legal obligations. I recall particularly the Wonderly brothers in the Siletz basin. One of them had the unique experience of having three houses destroyed in the time I knew him. The first, built in the creek bottom was washed away. His second, higher up, was demolished by a tremendous boulder which fate directed, fortunately, in the owner's absence. The third house was burned. His fourth house was home when I knew him.

C.P. Cronk, 1910-1911

In 1907, Stephen A. Douglas Puter, a timber-land broker from Eureka, California, wrote a book exposing his career in land fraud and drew national attention to Oregon's Lincoln County. Puter's book, written "in the dismal recesses of a prison cell," had a strong credibility, since Puter himself had been convicted of land fraud in a dramatic case that made headlines across the nation. He was indicted in Federal Court in Oregon, fled to Boston, was arrested by federal agents, provided evidence against his cronies, was incarcerated in the Multnomah County jail, and was pardoned by President Theodore Roosevelt. The journalists had a field day. In his book, Puter named names, cited specific places, and revealed the complex workings of the "Oregon land fraud ring." The book was a best seller and may have made Puter more money than some of his fraudulent dealings.

The subject of illegal acquisition of public lands is complex. The idea of wealthy capitalists stealing land from the government is guaranteed to provoke most people. In fact, the methods used by ranchers and timber companies to acquire government lands were generally within the letter, if not perhaps the spirit, of the law. As Puter points out, the safest and most reliable method of getting government timber land after the Timber and Stone Act of 1878 was for investors to buy up Timber and Stone Act claims. Puter and others went so far as to sponsor the original claimants, paying the fees for their 160 acres, and even paying their travel expenses to the land office. Employing subsidized claimants, or "dummies," was not ethical, but when the government brought J.N. Williamson and Dr. Van Gerstner of Crook County, Oregon, to trial for this practice in 1905, the court decided it was not illegal.[19] After this landmark case, the government generally declined to prosecute Timber and Stone Act cases in Oregon.

Cartoon included by Puter in *Looters of the Public Domain.*

Puter and his associates used three principal schemes in Oregon's Linn, Lane, and Lincoln counties. The first was to use dummy Timber and Stone Act claimants. This practice was widespread and not original to Puter's group. The second scheme—the state school section strategy—was more complex. The Territorial Act of 1848 set aside two sections in each township for state schools.[20] If the school sections were incorporated into Indian reservations, Carey Act irrigation projects, timber reserves, or other federal projects, the states would be "indemnified" or compensated for their lost lands with other lands from the public domain. The state could sell the right to claim these indemnity lands. The claimant was required to pay $2.50 an acre to the state and provide the legal description of state lands lost to the federal government. Puter bribed state officials in Salem to tamper with legal descriptions of lost state lands so that his "dummies" could claim them each several times.[21] A Marion County grand jury in 1905 estimated that 500,000 acres of state school land sales were fraudulent.[22]

The third scheme was Puter's original idea, and he explained it to his readers with considerable pride. The Organic Act of 1897 made it possible for homesteaders whose land was incorporated into federal projects, like the forest reserves, to exchange their lands for other unclaimed lands on the public domain. Investors bought the rights to the exchanges and could get valuable timber land in exchange for ordinary homestead land. Puter's twist on this legal practice was to find an isolated unsurveyed township on the Cascade Forest Reserve and invent fictional homestead claims in the township. Since the township was unsurveyed, General Land Office records were sketchy. With a few well-placed bribes he was able to turn spurious homestead filings on land near the Cascade summit into claims on Lincoln County timber land.[23]

One of Puter's best clients was Minneapolis timberman C.A. Smith. Puter helped Smith and his associate Frederick Kribs acquire thousands of acres in Oregon and Northern California. Smith was co-owner of the Smith-Powers Lumber Company in Coos Bay. Smith was also the owner of a 12,700 acre tract of old-growth timber south of Waldport usually called the Blodgett Tract. It was incorporated into the Siuslaw National Forest in 1941 as the Yachats Purchase Unit.

Smith, Kribs, and John DuBois assembled the Blodgett Tract by a variety of means. State school indemnity lands accounted for eleven full sections and six partial sections.[24] Smith and his associates used dubious Santa Fe Railroad scrip and Timber and Stone Act claims as well. The one person associated with the Blodgett Tract who was likely not tainted, ironically enough, was John W. Blodgett, for whom the tract was named. Blodgett bought the land from Smith as a whole parcel in 1917. Blodgett's agent, P.S. Brunley, warned Blodgett that Smith's titles to timberland were in doubt, and that the best thing for the "Pacific Coast Country" would be to "shut him out and shut him down."[25] Smith, Kribs, and DuBois were under indictment for many years, and eventually lost thousands of acres of disputed land. Smith himself lost 38 parcels of land with disputed title in Oregon, California, and Wisconsin totaling over 6,000 acres.[26]

C.A. Smith mill on Coos Bay. C.P. Cronk photo, 1910-1911.

The big cases of land fraud with celebrities like C.A. Smith made the best copy for the newspapers, but small operators were prosecuted as well.

> *...a number of old soldiers had filed on 160 acres each, thinking that the service they had given in the Army served as residence on the land. ...Willard Jones, who had sold a lot of timber land to some eastern friends had made a lot of money in commissions, had loaned some of these old soldiers a few hundred dollars and took mortgages on their claims, and...had been indicted for fraud [as a result]*
>
> A. W. Morgan, *Fifty Years in Siletz Timber*

Land fraud was not confined to the Oregon coast, of course. The Western states had the most public land for unscrupulous people to steal, but the Great Lakes states and the Middle Atlantic states also had their share of fraud.[27] The government responded by investigating and prosecuting, and the courts were generally cooperative. However, enforcement alone could not deal with the widespread violations of various federal land programs. Congress recognized that reform of the land laws was needed to preserve timber, watershed, and other natural resources on public forests.

As a result, Congress passed on March 2, 1891, "an Act to repeal Timber Culture laws and other purposes," generally known as the Creative Act. The new law repealed the much-abused Timber Culture Act and the Preemption Act. It ended government sale of large tracts of land by auction, and tightened up the requirements of the Homestead Act, the Desert Land Act, and the Free Timber Act.[28] Despite the Act's purpose of reforming existing laws, its most significant provision was Section 24, which created the Forest Reserve system across the U.S.

Section 24 That the President of the United States may, from time to time, set apart and reserve, in any State or Territory having public lands wholly or in part covered with timber or undergrowth, whether of commercial value or not, as public reservations, and the President shall, by public proclamation, declare the establishments of such reservations, and the limits thereof.

Act of March 2, 1891

Presidents Harrison and Cleveland set about creating forest reserves at a great pace, but there was little direction from Congress about the management of the reserves until the Organic Act of 1897 provided some direction for the Department of the Interior. The reserves created significant controversy almost from the beginning. Opponents typically included lumber operators, miners, and ranchers. Supporters included a mix of wealthy Easterners like E.H. Harriman, organizations like the American Association for the Advancement of Science, and individual conservationists.

As the forest reserves program continued, the politics became more complicated. Small loggers and lumbermen opposed the reserves, but large lumber companies like Weyerhaeuser supported the reserves. They hoped that the reserves would diminish the amount of timber available, and that their own private timber and would then increase in value. Sheep were excluded from the reserves, so sheep ranchers opposed them, but cattle and horses were allowed to graze, so cattle ranchers withheld their opinion. Advocates for Oregon's Cascade Forest Reserve, for example, included John Breckenridge Waldo and

William G. Steele—famous conservationists—and Stephen A.D. Puter—famous crook.[29]

One of the strongest critics of the forest reserve program was Oregon Senator Charles Fulton, who had himself been implicated in land fraud cases. After several unsuccessful attempts, Fulton introduced legislation that would end the President's power to create forest reserves in 1907. The Fulton Amendment was passed and was to become law on March 7, 1907. Before the new law took effect, however, Chief Forester Gifford Pinchot and his staff hastily drew boundaries for 17 new forest reserves containing 16,000,000 acres. President Theodore Roosevelt signed the new "Midnight" Reserves into existence before the Fulton Amendment became law, creating in Oregon the Blue Mountains, Cascade, Coquille, Imnaha, Tillamook, and Umpqua reserves.

The Tillamook Forest Reserve included the Hebo area, and the Umpqua Forest Reserve included coastal lands near the Umpqua River. According to the author of *A History of the Siuslaw National Forest, Oregon, as of December 31, 1939*, the creation of these reserves was not related to any local issue. There was little notice of the new reserves in the local or state-wide newspapers. In November of 1907, eight months after President Roosevelt had created the "Midnight Reserves," Senator Fulton spoke in Toledo, Oregon, but did not mention the two new reserves in his speech.[30] Nevertheless, Puter's much-publicized adventures with the law, and his book *Looters of the Public Domain*, had drawn attention to the central Oregon coast as early as 1905. Two of the public lands areas in Oregon that Puter singled out as hotbeds of fraud were the central coast and the Blue Mountains. These areas accounted for four of the six new reserves in Oregon formed early in March, 1907.

NOTES

1. Stephen Dow Beckham, Katherine Anne Toepel, and Rick Minor, *Cultural Resource Overview of the Siuslaw National Forest, Western Oregon* (Corvallis, OR: Siuslaw NF, 1982) 62. Beckham's excellent synthesis of ethnographic and historical information serves as a basis for this section of chapter 1.
2. Consultation with David M. Petrie, Cultural Director, Confederated Tribes of Coos, Lower Umpqua and Siuslaw Indians.
3. Beckham, 1982, 122-123.
4. For history of coastal and Willamette Valley Indians in this period see Stephen Dow Beckham, *Requiem for A People: the Rogue Indians and the Frontiersmen* (Norman, OK: University of Oklahoma Press, 1971) and Stephen Dow Beckham, *The Indians of Western Oregon, This Land was Theirs* (Coos Bay, OR: Arago Books, 1977).
5. Siletz and Grand Ronde figures from Beckham 1982, 225; Alsea figures from Marjorie H. Hays, *The Land That Kept its Promise* (Newport, OR: Lincoln County Historical Society) 36.
6. Beckham, 1982, 235.
7. J.P. Kinney, *A Continent Lost, A Civilization Won* (Baltimore, MD: John Hopkins, 1936) 355-356.
8. Beckham, 1982, 231.
9. *A History of the Siuslaw National Forest, Oregon, as of December 31, 1939* (on file, Waldport, OR: Siuslaw NF, 1939) 10 **(hereafter cited as "*History*")**; Beckham 1982, 233.
10. David D. Fagan, *History of Benton County, Oregon* (Portland, OR: A.G. Walling, 1885) 462.
11. Richard A. Price, *Newport, Oregon 1866-1936* (Newport, OR: Lincoln County Historical Society, 1975) 8.
12. "*History*," 12.
13. C. Frank Grant, "The Grants of Grant Valley" (on file, Waldport, OR: Siuslaw NF, 1990) 14.
14. Beckham, 1982, 241.
15. "*History*," 14.
16. Beckham, 1982, 237.
17. Beckham, 1982, 238.
18. "*History*," 48.
19. S.A.D. Puter, *Looters of the Public Domain* (New York, NY: Arno, 1975 reprint) 339-345.
20. James O'Callahan, *Disposition of the Public Lands in Oregon* (New York, NY: Arno, 1979) 64.
21. Puter, 316.
22. Blodgett Papers, Brumley to Blodgett, December 26, 1918; *Oregon Journal,* December 22, 1918.
23. Puter, 46-67.
24. Ward Tonsfeldt, "History of the Blodgett Tract" (on file, Waldport, OR: Siuslaw NF, 1988) 16.
25. Blodgett Papers, Brumley to Blodgett, April 14, 1915.
26. U.S. Bureau of Corporations, *The Lumber Industry* (Washington, DC: USGPO, 1914) vol. 2, 57.
27. See *The Lumber Industry,* vol. 1 for a general account.
28. For discussions of this significant piece of legislation, see Samuel T. Dana, *Forest and Range Policy* (New York, NY: McGraw Hill, 1956) 98-119; Lawrence Rakestraw, "A History of Forest Conservation in the Pacific Northwest" (unpub. Dissert.: University of Washington, 1955); Gerald Williams, *USDA Forest Service: the First Century* (Washington, DC: USGPO, 2000) 8-25.

29 Puter, 427; see also Lawrence Rakestraw, *History of the Willamette National Forest* (Eugene, OR: USDA-FS, 1975) 2.

30 "*History*," 2.

CHAPTER TWO

THE SIUSLAW NATIONAL FOREST

FOREST RESERVES TO NATIONAL FOREST

President Theodore Roosevelt—known for his abiding commitment to conservation—created the Umpqua and Tillamook Forest Reserves on March 2, 1907. The political atmosphere in Washington, DC was unusually heavy at the time, for Oregon's Senator Charles Fulton had finally managed to get legislation through Congress that would eclipse the President's ability to create new forest reserves. The Fulton Amendment was to become law on March 7. Roosevelt's friend, Chief Forester Gifford Pinchot, had prepared rather hastily-drawn maps of new reserves proposed for the West. Roosevelt signed papers to create the new reserves as quickly as he could. Some were signed late at night in the White House offices—so the term "Midnight Reserves" is applied to the 17 new reserves created in the first week of March, 1907.

> **Now therefore, I, THEODORE ROOSEVELT, President of the United States of America, by virtue of the power vested in me by section twenty-four of the aforesaid act of Congress [Act of March 3, 1891] do proclaim that there are hereby reserved from entry or settlement and set apart as a Public Reservation, for the use and benefit of the people all the tracts of land in the State of Oregon, shown as the Umpqua Forest Reserve on the diagram forming a part hereof;**
>
> **Umpqua Forest Reserve Proclamation, March 2, 1907**

Fourteen months later, on June 30, 1908, Roosevelt combined the Tillamook Forest Reserve and the coastal part of the Umpqua Forest Reserve into the new Siuslaw National Forest. In 1908, the distinction between forest reserve and national forest was becoming confusing. The forest reserves dated back to 1891, when the Creative Act enabled the President to designate forest reserves. The reserves were managed by the General Land Office (GLO) of the Department of the Interior. On February 1, 1905, Theodore Roosevelt and Gifford Pinchot shifted the responsibility for the reserves to the Department of Agriculture's Forestry Branch. On July 1, the Forestry Branch became the Forest Service. On March 4, 1907, all forest reserves became national forests.

Ranger George McCaskie (seated plaid shirt) and staff.

The Tillamook and Umpqua Reserves were created on March 2, 1907, as forest reserves, then became national forests on March 4, 1907, and finally became the Siuslaw National Forest fourteen months later. The distinction between forest reserves and national forests may appear to be a bureaucratic quibble, but the two organizations had profoundly different philosophies and operating policies.

The GLO Bureau of Forestry—organized after the Organic Act of 1897—was primarily concerned with preserving the reserves. The Bureau operated through a system of politically appointed local rangers. Public relations and commitment to service were not always priorities. For example, settlers could obtain timber for their own use only if they met stringent citizenship and residence requirements or were declared destitute. Commercial use of timber involved a complicated procedure intended to deter applicants. First the mill owner had to meet residency requirements, then apply in writing to purchase a tract of his choice, then wait for the local office of the Bureau to inspect it, then negotiate a price, then wait for the Bureau to mark it, then wait for Washington to approve it. At that point, the sale was advertised in local newspapers for 30 days of open bidding, and the timber sold to the highest bidder.[1] Mill owners could use this system to ensure that a competitor could not get public timber. Since the local Bureau of Forestry managers were political appointments and not necessarily professional foresters, opportunities for influence and favoritism abounded.

Forest Service staff examines stump, Berbe-Wright Homestead. C.P. Cronk photo, 1910-1911.

The Forest Service, on the other hand, held competitive examinations for administrative positions and prided itself on professional forestry. In *The Use of the National Forests*, Gifford Pinchot wrote a policy manual aimed at convincing the public that the Forest Service was dedicated to seeing that all resources in the national forest were available for use. For example, *The Use Book* has this to say about timber sales: "The timber is there first of all to be used. The more it is used, the better. Far from being locked up, it is on the contrary opened up, and opened up on fair terms to all alike."[2] The actual policy that the Forest Service developed for commercial timber sales was a little more complicated than *The Use Book* suggests, but the public found the Forest Service approach more palatable than that of the Bureau of Forestry.

The new agency was committed to open opportunity for grazing rights and timber sales on the national forests. The Forest Homestead Act of 1906 ensured that some homestead land would be available on the national forests, and mining laws allowed mineral claims. Legislation passed in 1906 required ten percent (later 25 percent) of net receipts from national forest grazing fees and timber sales to go to local governments in lieu of taxes. These measures improved the public's opinion of the national forest program.[3]

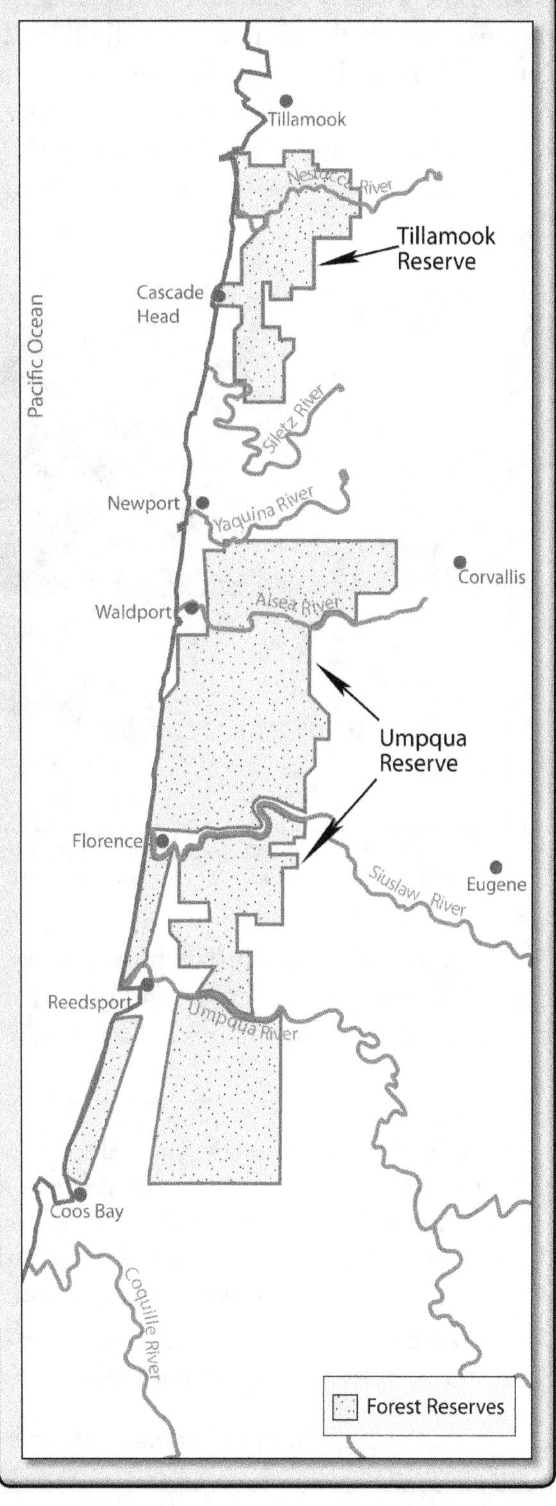

It is hereby ordered that on and after July 1, 1908, the land within the boundaries shown on the attached diagram, herefore set apart, reserved, and proclaimed as the Tillamook National Forest, and parts of the Umpqua National Forest shall be known as the Siuslaw National Forest.

Theodore Roosevelt
Executive Order,
Siuslaw National Forest
June 30, 1908

The two Midnight Reserves—the Tillamook and the Umpqua—were hastily conceived on March 2, 1907. Combining the Tillamook with the "Coast Range Umpqua" to form the Siuslaw National Forest was a logical step and facilitated administration. However, the result was not especially tidy. The old Tillamook Reserve became the Hebo Ranger District. It was cut off from the center of the Forest by the 25 mile wide Siletz River basin, which was largely private timber land and Siletz Indian allotments. South of the Alsea River was the Waldport Ranger District, then south of that was the Florence Ranger District, and then the Gardiner Ranger District. The Supervisors Office was in Eugene.

Supplies to Heceta Head area were brought in by boat before roads and bridges were built. Photo ca. 1892, lightstation under construction.

Getting around the Siuslaw took a major effort. With the exception of Hebo, the original four ranger districts all had their district headquarters on the coast. This made sense because travel by water was easier than by road or trail.

Among early administrative problems which faced the new Supervisor in 1907 was that of transportation. Roads were still non-existent and the broad estuaries of the main rivers, into which tidewater flowed inland some 20 miles were the obvious avenues of communication. Rapid transit in those days was envisioned by Forest Assistant Cockroft as follows:

> **"When one can jump into a boat and ride 25 miles in three hours, do his day's work and come back, there is a great deal of time to be saved!"**

A History of the Siuslaw National Forest, Oregon, as of December 31, 1939

The Siuslaw set about obtaining boats immediately for use on the Alsea, Siuslaw, Smith, and Umpqua rivers. The first were 20-foot launches built at Acme (now Cushman), near Florence, by Martin Noffsinger for $60 each. One of these boats stayed on the Siuslaw River, and the second one was stationed on the Alsea. The Forest ordered two more launches from a boat builder in Gardiner. These operated on the Smith and Umpqua rivers. Four 26-foot scows were built for the launches to tow, and all eight boats were in use by 1908. After ten years' service the original fleet was replaced with three larger motorboats, the *Umpqua*, the *Siuslaw*, and the *Alsea*. These operated into the 1920s, when roads and automobiles became more practical, and the boats could be decently disposed as surplus property.[4]

The duties of Forest Service staff in the early decades included forest inspection, fire suppression, planting, and other management tasks. Corydon P. Cronk passed his examination for Assistant Forest Ranger in 1910 and came to work on the Hebo Ranger District. Cronk was an enthusiastic photographer and left a collection of photos, as well as a chronicle of his work.

Corydon P. Cronk was Assistant Ranger on Hebo 1910-1911.

Cronk's adventures on the Siuslaw in 1910 and 1911 included packing with burros. Forest Supervisor Anson Cohoon had purchased the burros for the Forest, since they could work where there were "no roads, few trails, and no pasturage." When he was not delivering burros, Cronk spent his time fighting fires, checking homestead claims, and packing supplies to fire crews and planting crews.

Ranger District boat, probably on the Alsea River.

In the late summer of 1910 there was posted in the lobby of the Eugene post office an announcement that on October 24 there would be a civil service examination for Assistant Forest Ranger, U.S. Forest Service. On the appointed day, I, along with 8 or 10 others, appeared. The exam was divided into two parts. On the first day field tests were given; on the second, written ones.

The high point of the [examination] was the horse packing test—loading properly and tying a hitch all within 15 minutes. The items strewn all over the stable floor consisted of an ax, shovel, mattock, cross-cut saw, blankets, cooking utensils, eating utensils, and empty suitcase, a sheet iron heating stove, and a 50-pound bag of salt. In the midst were two canvas panniers and a X-frame pack saddle. No one of the devil's disciples could have contrived a more cunning assembly of objects to be effectively distributed on a horse's back or have arranged them more confusedly on the stable floor.

C.P. Cronk, 1910-1911

On a rainy day about November 1, 1910, I made the acquaintance of my two traveling companions, the mother, May, and the daughter, Fanny. We started out of Eugene in style and ease....We continued toward the coast as far as Indian Creek. Here I picked the rest of the party, "Vic," the biggest and most even-tempered of our burros, and "Bubbles," the smartest and smallest....From the end of the ridge trail at the Corvallis-Waldport road we turned east, there being no road along the coast. From Corvallis we went north to Sheridan and along the road to Willamina to Dolph and Hebo, then up the mountain to the ranger station. This was approximately 225 miles and 22 days from Eugene.

C.P. Cronk, 1910-1911

C.P. Cronk packing with burros.

I had borrowed a boat to go up the Siletz River to examine a couple of homestead claims. I made my way up the river to my objectives, but on the way back I found the incoming tide so strong it took me about twice the normal time to get back to Kernville. The next morning the tide was so high I couldn't get away from Kernville until afternoon. I made my way to Drift Creek, but there the Indian woman would not ferry me across until the tide started in again, which I couldn't blame her for. After crossing late in the afternoon I hit the Schooner Creek trail, which was worn down about four inches or more through the turf and was then under about a foot of water from the storm tides. Suddenly, pack and all, I plunged into a drainage ditch. I scrambled up the other side very wet, but it didn't bother me very much as I had left a boat at Schooner Creek when I came over the day before, and I knew I could get dried off at Taft where I would spend the night. But when I reached Schooner Creek, I discovered someone had taken the boat and rowed it across the creek. As darkness was fast approaching, I started looking for shelter and came upon a group of summer cottages. I didn't want to break into one, but I did need to get my clothes dried...So I entered one that had blankets hanging on a wire, and a pile of rutabagas. I ate the raw rutabagas for supper and breakfast. Before leaving I left the owner a note asking him to let me know the cost of a new lock and I would pay. It was summer before I got there again. He had fixed the lock and would take no pay.

C.P. Cronk, 1910-1911

In addition to its isolation, the Siuslaw also has geographical diversity. The Forest includes the coast, which is rare among national forests. The sand dunes extending south from Florence to Coos Bay, and near Sand Lake on the Hebo Ranger District, are also unusual. Inland, the Forest has dense stands of Douglas fir, common to other national forests west of the Cascades. Near the coast, Sitka spruce, western hemlock, shore pine, and cascara are found in many stands. Heceta Head is another unusual feature for a national forest. Geographical points of interest also include promontories like Marys Peak, Cape Perpetua, and Cascade Head.

Heceta Head lightstation, 1910.

The Heceta Head lightstation antedates the creation of the Forest. It was one of the last lightstations built on the Oregon coast. In 1892 the federal Lighthouse Board began construction of the Heceta Head complex. Construction was difficult on this exposed portion of the coast, necessitating delivery of supplies by wagon when possible and by floating lumber through the surf. The beacon was complete and in service by the spring of 1894. The buildings at Heceta included a Head Keeper's house, a duplex for two Assistants, barn, the lighthouse itself, and two oil houses.

The lightstation was supplied from the sea by the Life Saving Service tender *Rose* until roads improved. Through the 1910s, the lightstation staff and neighbors on Cape Creek were an isolated community. In 1910, the Lighthouse Service succeeded the Lighthouse Board, and in 1939, the Coast Guard succeeded the Lighthouse Service as

The lumber came in on the beach. I mean everything in those days came by water one way or another. It was thrown over the side and floated in and people salvaged it, or the materials came in a small boat and were collected. The supplies for the lighthouse were brought in a small boat. The lighthouse tenders would lay-to out there beyond the breakers, then row the supplies in.

John Bray, Cape Creek homestead family, 1997 Interview

Life Saving Service tender *Rose*.

the operator of aids to navigation throughout the U.S. The Coast Guard sold the keeper's house, which was dismantled and salvaged. During World War II, the Coast Guard patrolled the beach with soldiers and guard dogs. In 1963 the light was automated, and the Coast Guard turned the service buildings over to the Siuslaw National Forest. The Forest and Oregon State Parks jointly manage Heceta Head. The Forest leased the buildings to Lane Community College from 1970 to 1995. The college operated a field school there and conducted some classes. In 1978 the lightstation was listed in the National Register of Historic Places. As a heritage resource, the complex needed restoration and more public access. The Forest now manages the buildings under a special use permit as the Heceta Lighthouse Bed and Breakfast. Revenues support restoration and maintenance.

Assistant Keeper Robert DeRoy and wife Jenny.

Another prominent headland on the coast is Cape Perpetua. Acting Forest Superintendent J. Roy Harvey closed the Cape to homestead entry in 1914.[5] After 1932, the Civilian Conservation Corps prepared a recreation plan for the "Perpetua-Heceta Recreational Unit." In 1933 the Forest proposed that the area inland from the Cape be set aside as an official Forest Service Natural Area preserving the old-growth Sitka spruce-Western hemlock forest type. E.L. Kolbe and the CCC argued for the recreational potential of the Cape, which led to the formation of the Cape Perpetua Natural Area and the Perpetua Picnic Park and Camp. These became the Cape Perpetua Scenic Area in 1962.

Head Keeper Clifford B. "Cap" Hermann and "Mom" Hermann.

Cascade Head and the Salmon River estuary.

Cascade Head, near the Salmon River estuary, had a similar history, but it remains primarily a research forest. This conspicuous headland was first set aside and protected as an example of the Sitka spruce-Western hemlock forest type. Legislation in 1934 designated 6,417 acres including the promontory and nearby forest as the Cascade Head Experimental Forest. A residence, storage building, and garage were built in 1936 for the field supervisor on the site. Later the Experimental Forest was expanded to 11,890 acres.

In 1974 Congress established the 9,670-acre Cascade Head Scenic Research Area that includes the western half of the Experimental Forest and the Salmon River

Cascade Head Experimental Forest headquarters.

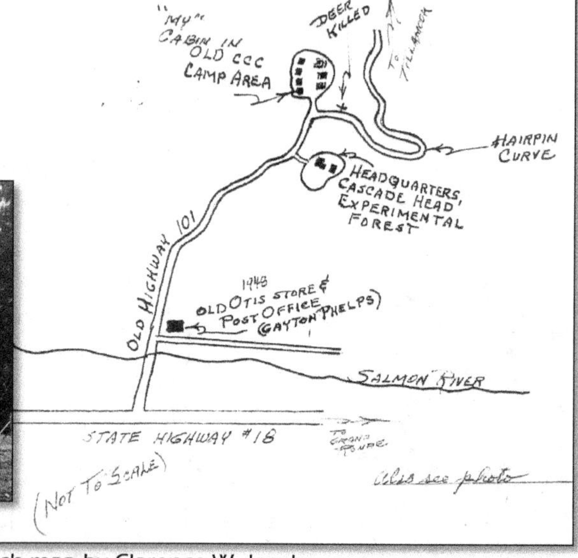

Sketch map by Clarence W. Jacobs.

estuary. In 1980 the entire area was designated a Biosphere Reserve as part of the United Nations Biosphere Reserve system. The Siuslaw and the USDA Forest Service Pacific Northwest Research Station manage the experimental forest and scenic research area jointly. Research partners include The Nature Conservancy, state and private universities in Oregon and Washington, Oregon Department of Fish and Wildlife, Oregon Department of Agriculture, National Aeronautic and Space Administration, Environmental Protection Agency, and National Marine Fisheries Service.

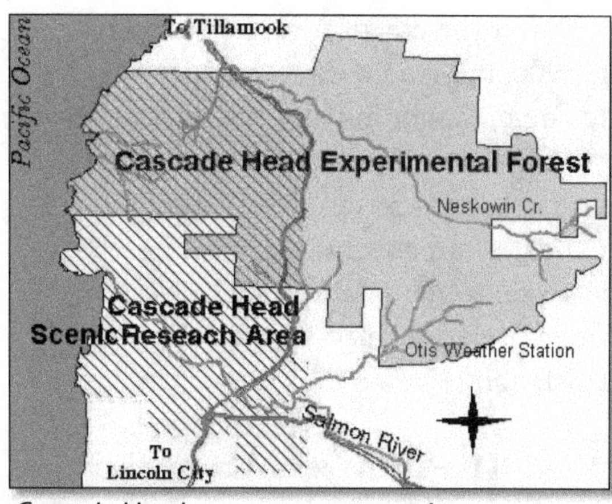

Cascade Head management complex.

Gifford Pinchot's decision to include the extensive sand dunes between Florence and Coos Bay in the Umpqua Forest Reserve remains something of a mystery. The area is a fascinating landscape, but it does not meet any ordinary criteria for forest land. The Forest made dogged attempts to stabilize the dunes by planting willows, pines, European beach grass, and Scotch broom. The large lakes immediately east of the dunes were popular with tourists, especially after the Southern Pacific Railroad provided rail service for passengers in 1916. But the dunes had little appeal until motor vehicle sports became popular in the years after World War II. Dune buggy enthusiasts from Oregon, Washington, and California gathered to drive their home-made vehicles through the sand dunes.

In 1959 Oregon Senator Richard Neuberger proposed to make the dunes a National Seashore and bring it under the administration of the National Park Service, a branch of the Department of the Interior. The Forest Service did not want to lose control of what was becoming an important recreation draw for the Siuslaw. In a compromise with the Department of the Interior, the dunes became the Oregon Dunes National Recreation Area in 1972 and remained part of the Siuslaw National Forest.

Dedication ceremony, Oregon Dunes National Recreation Area, 1972.

ADDITIONS TO THE SIUSLAW

After the creation of the Forest in 1908, the land base remained dynamic, expanding and contracting in small increments to reflect exchanges, purchases, and certain legislative mandates. In general, this process was common to national forests in western Oregon, and enabled by the following legislation:

> **1911—The Weeks Act** enabled national forests to purchase lands within their boundaries to improve management. Subsequent amendments to the Weeks Act expanded its scope.
>
> **1916—The Chamberlain-Ferris Act** returned the Oregon and California Railroad grant lands to the Department of the Interior and created the O&C lands checkerboard of alternate sections across western and southern Oregon.
>
> **1922—The General Exchange Act** enabled national forests to exchange lands with other landowners to consolidate holdings or for other management purposes.

Each of these federal laws represented the results of months, and sometimes years, of deliberation and compromise between parties and interest groups in Washington, DC.

The municipal watersheds of Corvallis, Philomath, and Dallas became the first major acquisition for the Siuslaw. This occurred February 11, 1920, and

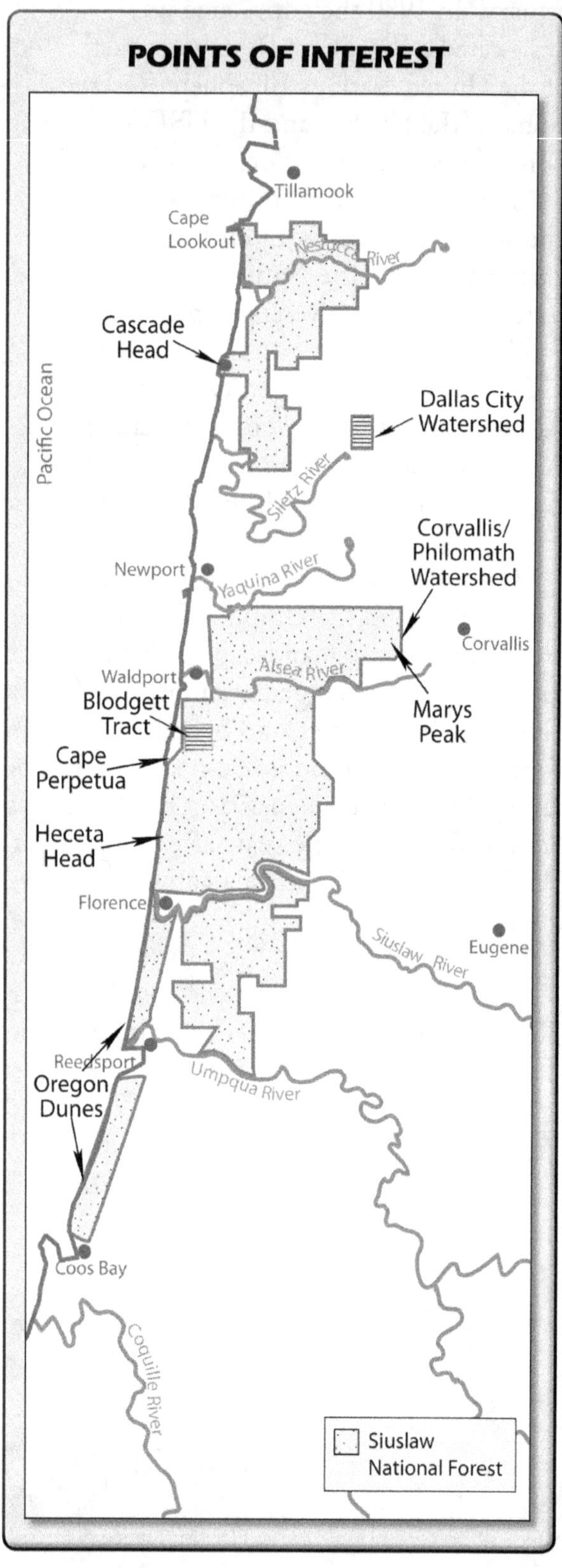

added two tracts totaling 2,880 acres. The Dallas watershed consisted of 1,160 acres in T 7 S, R 6 W, and the Corvallis-Philomath watershed consisted of 1,720 acres in T 12 S, R 7 W. Both tracts were former O&C lands. Concerned citizens of the three cities promoted the exchange.[6] The Dallas municipal watershed remains an isolated tract of Siuslaw National Forest land separated from the rest of the Forest by 30 miles. The Corvallis municipal watershed is located on the east slope of Marys Peak and led to other Siuslaw acquisitions in this area.

The second major acquisition was a continuation of the Marys Peak purchases. This consisted of exchanges and Weeks Act purchases totaling 12,480 acres in several transactions. Purchases began in 1936 with the Forest Reservation Commission's approval of the projects and continued through 1940. The largest landowner in the area was the A.C. Spaulding Lumber Company. The motivation for the purchase was additional watershed protection. Corvallis residents asked that the Forest Service acquire the lands to prevent excessive logging. Some of the land had been logged, but much had merchantable timber remaining.[7] Additional purchases made under the terms of the Weeks Act totaled 7,315 acres.

The third major acquisition was the complicated land exchange that occurred as a result of New Deal rural land programs during the Depression. These programs included the National Industrial Recovery Act, the Agricultural Adjustment Administration, Western Oregon Scattered Settlers Project, the Farm Security Administration, Bureau of Agricultural Economics, and the Soil Conservation Service. The programs acquired 69,482 acres of abandoned lands, low-income farm lands, and cut-over timber land in or adjacent to the Siuslaw. All of the purchased lands that were not originally O&C lands were added to the Siuslaw in two transfers in 1940.

The New Deal rural lands programs were controversial in their own time, as the bewildering succession of agencies implies. They were controversial in later times as well. The programs were designed for poor rural areas in Appalachia and the Dust Bowl states. They were an uncomfortable fit in the West, where land values were calculated by standing timber, and the timber cycle was as short as 30 years. Siuslaw National Forest Supervisor Ralph Shelley was detailed to run the program for the government in western Oregon. He was an excellent administrator and knew and sympathized with the impoverished "scattered settlers" throughout the region.

Another major acquisition for the Siuslaw was the Blodgett Tract, 12,700 acres of cut-over and burned land once owned by timber investor John Blodgett. Later, the Blodgett Tract was owned by the U.S. Spruce Production Corporation, a government corporation formed in 1919. The tract was located south of Waldport and north of the Yachats River.

The Blodgett Tract was arguably the most controversial piece of timber land on the entire coast. Lumberman A.C. Smith and his associate Frederick Krebs assembled the tract from the public domain by dubious means, then sold it to John Blodgett in 1916. Blodgett in turn sold it to the U.S. Army under duress in 1918. No one would buy it from the Army, although the Pacific Spruce Company negotiated a purchase agreement with the Army, logged it, and abandoned it. Lincoln County could not collect taxes because it was owned by a federal corporation, which was itself in trouble with Congress at the time. In 1936 the Blodgett Tract ignited and burned in a long and expensive forest fire. When the Siuslaw agreed to buy the tract in 1941, all of the ownership and management problems were resolved.

When the Oregon Dunes NRA was formed in 1972, the Siuslaw began a program to acquire lands to consolidate this area. Through the 1980s, over 10,000 acres of land have come into the Forest. Riparian lands on several streams important for anadromous fish have been acquired by the forest in recent years.

THE ELLIOTT STATE FOREST

The Territorial Act of 1848 designated sections 16 and 36 in each Oregon township as state lands for funding education. As Oregon grew, the state sold these school sections to finance public schools. Indian reservations, forest reserves, and railroad and wagon road land grants created situations in which the state sections could no longer be sold or managed for the state's needs. The first response to this situation was exchanging individual state school sections for unclaimed sections of the public domain. However, this presented excellent opportunities for land fraud.

The second strategy was to exchange all the school sections on federal reserves for other land of equal value in a continuous tract. In 1912, State Forester Francis Elliott and Governor Oswald West formulated the concept of trading scattered school lands within national forests for a block of national forest land, thereby making the state lands usable, and simultaneously solving the land fraud problem.[8] Since the proposal would make the scattered sections of state land much more valuable as a continuous tract, easily logged, the plan favored the state. The Oregon Legislature approved the plan in 1919, and negotiations continued between the state and the Forest Service. In 1924, three national forest tracts were proposed as potential exchanges for 37,000 acres of state lands in the national forests of eastern and central Oregon, and 33,000 acres in western Oregon.

The three government tracts were the Millicoma Tract, 70,000 acres in Coos and Douglas counties on the Siuslaw; the Table Mountain Tract, 70,000 acres in Lincoln County on the Siuslaw; and the Blowout Creek Tract, 70,000 acres on the Cascade National Forest. The timber on the tracts varied, as did soils, elevations, and other elements. The state opted for the Millicoma Tract, but the Forest Service and the state disagreed about an additional 7,000 acres needed to complete the deal. The Forest Service proposed that the state take 7,000 acres of the sand dunes on the coast south of Florence. The state was not inclined towards taking the sand dunes but would accept 7,000 acres of O&C lands adjacent to the tract. President Calvin Coolidge transfered 6,818 acres of O&C lands to Oregon in 1927.

In 1929 the agreement was final, and Oregon owned the former Siuslaw lands south of the Umpqua River. The new state forest received some help with roads, trails, lookouts and other infrastructure from the Civilian Conservation Corps, which operated camps near Reedsport and at Loon Lake. Elliott State Forest was the first of the Oregon state forests, but several others followed in subsequent years. As a solution to the school section problem, it was a great success, as the timber on the Elliott has provided a continuous source of revenue for the state.

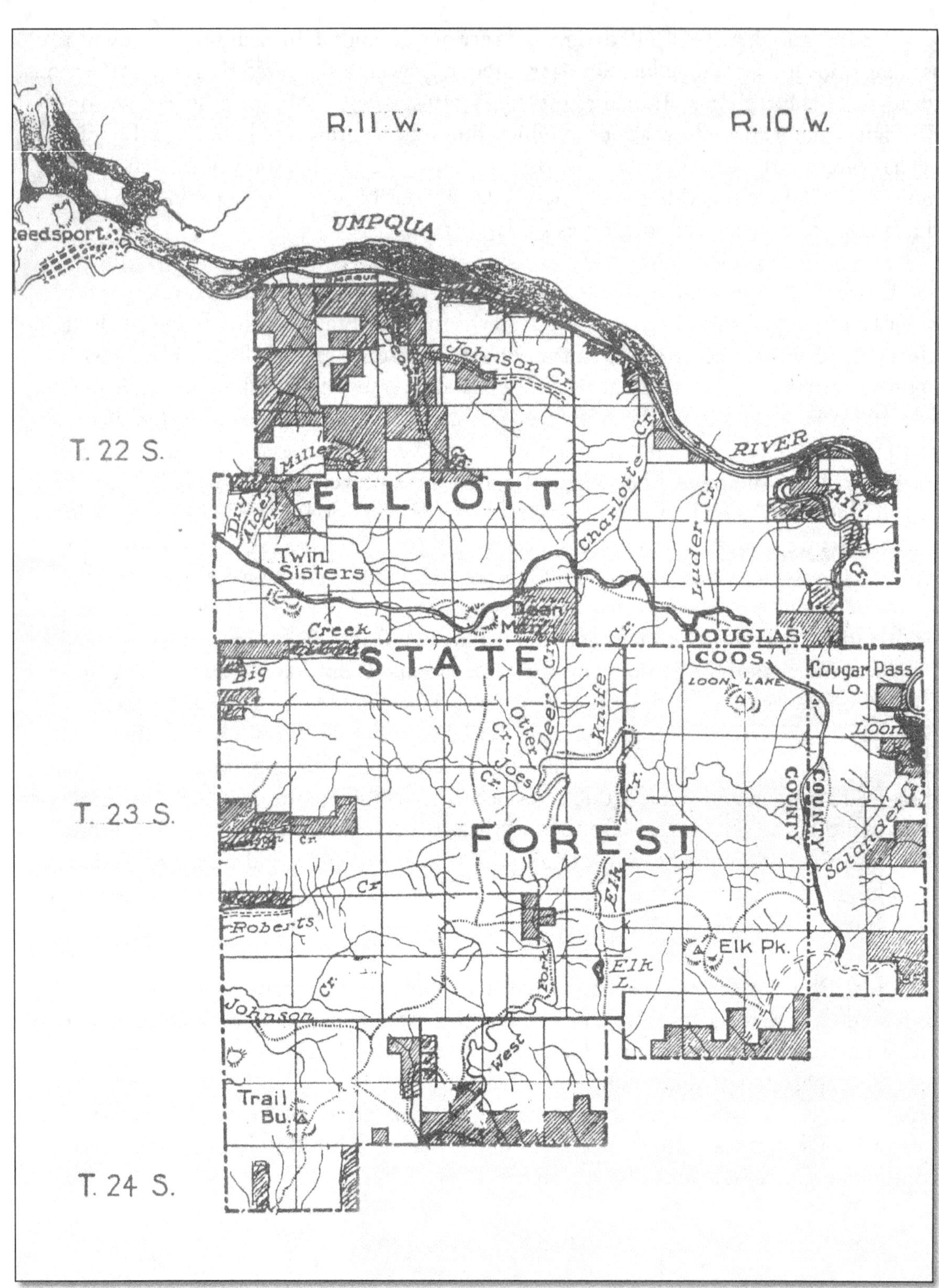

Elliott State Forest 1935.

In the years before World War II Rangers and Forest Supervisors had to deal with poor communications and difficult travel conditions. The Siuslaw was dispersed geographically along 200 miles of coast. Since the Supervisors Office was in Eugene, the ranger districts had a degree of separation and autonomy that was unusual. Among Forest Supervisors, Ralph S. Shelley had the longest tenure, leading the Forest from 1918 until 1938. He was credited with an intimate knowledge of the Forest and acquaintance with settlers in all parts. Other names that appear in early Siuslaw documents are Supervisor Anson Cohoon (1908-1913), Mapleton and Waldport Ranger Edward S. Kerby (1920-1945), Hebo Ranger Rolfe Anderson (1943-1967), Supervisor Rex Wakefield (1952-1962), and others. In more recent times, Forest Supervisor F. Dale Roberston (1973-1976) went on to become the 12th Chief of the Forest Service (1987-1993). Supervisors James Overbay and James Furnish also served in Washington, DC.

George T. McCaskie, Jr., Ranger at Florence.

Trail crew. C.P. Cronk photo, 1910-1911.

Dear Ralph [Shelley]:

I will never forget my first trip with you and Ed Kerby a long time ago. What a revelation it was to an inlandlubber: great, rolling shadowy sand dunes gritting the molars of the traveler and everlasting war with windcarved *picea* and Japanese *contorta*. Yes, and rhododendron trees, salal, *vaccinium* taller than the highest Siuslaw latrine....

Forest Inspector Fred W. Cleator

SIUSLAW FORESTERS THROUGH THE YEARS...

Robert Aufderheide was Ranger on the Hebo District 1937-1940.

C.W. Jacobs held several positions in the Forest during the 1950s and 1960s. He left us an excellent account of those years in his memoirs.

F. Dale Robertson (right) became 12th Chief of the Forest Service. Pictured here with Charlie Severson in the Washington office, 1989.

Tom Thompson, Forest Supervisor, 1987-1992.

James Furnish, Forest Supervisor, 1992-1999.

NOTES

1 *Forest Reserve Manual* (Washington, DC: USGPO, 1902) 14-15.

2 Gifford Pinchot, *The Use of the National Forests* (Washington, DC: USGPO, 1907) 12.

3 A good discussion of the Forest Service at its origin in 1905 can be found in Gerald W. Williams, *The USDA Forest Service, The First Century* (Washington, DC: USGPO, 2005) 17ff.

4 *A History of the Siuslaw National Forest, Oregon, as of December 31, 1939* (on file, Waldport, OR: Siuslaw NF, 1939) 32 (**hereafter cited as "*History*"**).

5 Both Cape Perpetua (Lincoln County) and Heceta Head (Lane County) have a Cape Creek adjacent to them.

6 "*History*", 27.

7 "*History*", 28.; Personal communication, Ken McCall, 2008

8 Jerry Phillips, *Caulked Boots and Cheese Sandwiches: A Forester's History of Oregon's First State Forest* (Coos Bay, OR: 1997) 2.

CHAPTER THREE

THE FOREST AND THE TREES

MANAGING THE FOREST IN 1908

In 1919, a few years after its formation, the Siuslaw National Forest contained within its boundaries 833,441 acres of land. Fully one third—280,745 acres—was alienated land owned by settlers, timber companies, and other private parties. About 2,500 people were living on homesteads within the boundaries. Sixty-seven thousand acres of the land in the new Forest was classified under the terms of the June 11, 1906, forest homestead program. The remaining 485,637 acres consisted of the following categories:

Coniferous timber land	370,013 acres
Deciduous woodland	58,019 acres
Burned forest	14,341 acres
Brush	9,795 acres
Grasslands	-0- acres
Barren land	16,324 acres
Unclassified (1919)	17,143 acres[1]

Forest road in representative stand of mature trees.

In *The Use of the National Forests* Gifford Pinchot had defined the job of the Forest Service as "forestry," which he further defined as "to protect and grow wood." Pinchot's definition would scarcely please academics or most professional foresters, but it was intended for an audience of skeptics who were concerned about the federal government taking over vast tracts of forest land and imposing new rules.

Natural regeneration in old burn, Hebo District.

PROTECTING THE FOREST

Dense stand of spruce and western hemlock.

Protecting the forest in the early years meant protecting it from fire, trespass, and unlawful entry. The first forest supervisors and district rangers did this by taking measures to detect and control fires, and to spread the gospel of fire prevention. Early accounts of forest management on the Siuslaw do not mention timber trespass as a serious concern. There were apparently plenty of trees to go around.

> **In my time on the Siuslaw there was probably no other National Forest so much concerned with people—people who were living in the area, and people who visited it from the Willamette Valley. There were settlers who owned their land, those in the process of fulfilling the process of homesteading, and absentee owners who had taken up land under the terms of the Timber and Stone Act. There were also the "timber homesteads," often fraudulent, some of which had cabins not much larger than a doghouse.**
>
> **C.P. Cronk, 1910-1911**

Unlawful occupation of Forest lands was another matter, however. When the Umpqua and Tillamook Forest Reserves were established in 1907 lands within the boundaries were no longer open to settlement.

However, the Forest Homestead Act of June 11, 1906, re-opened the lands to more homesteading after 1908 if the lands could be shown to have any potential for agriculture. Forest managers on the Siuslaw did not believe that any of the lands not already homesteaded were suitable for agriculture, so they closed the Forest to homesteading in 1911. Pressure from the Secretary of Agriculture required them to re-open the Forest in 1913. A flurry of homestead claims followed but gradually diminished until Forest Supervisor Ralph Shelley closed the Siuslaw to forest homestead claims once again in 1916.

Forest homestead cabin in dense timber.

Except during the height of the fire season, much of my time was spent examining and reporting on homestead and "June 11" [1906] claims. The Siuslaw National Forest had more "June 11" or Forest Homestead claims than any other National Forest, and examining them was a major assignment for me all the time I was on the Forest.

C.P. Cronk, 1910-1911

GROWING TREES

Gifford Pinchot's second charge to the agency he had created was to "grow trees." This was closer to the common view of forestry, and also closer to what the graduates of the new forestry programs at colleges and universities probably expected. The most important element of this was reforestation. Forest fires had burned over much of the central coast in the nineteenth century, and many of these burned areas had produced stands of second-growth conifers through natural regeneration after the fires. Some areas had not, however, and the Forest Service set about planting trees in these places soon after 1908. Planting techniques included walnuts planted with dibbles and seeds scattered on the snow. C.P. Cronk mentions packing supplies by burro to Mt. Hebo to keep a planting crew fed in the winter of 1910-1911.

Hebo District crew planting walnuts with dibbles. C.P. Cronk photo, 1910-1911.

Need for reforestation was immediately apparent [in 1908]. It began in 1908 in the Mt. Hebo area, which was... denuded of tree growth, with the planting of 2 ½ acres. W.H. Gibbons was in charge of this early work and 19 ½ acres were planted in 1909. H.M. Johnson came in the fall of 1912 and continued in general charge of the planting work until 1920.

A History of the Siuslaw National Forest, Oregon, as of December 31, 1939

The second growth fir grows more rapidly than the old-growth did, so that some of it is as much as three feet in diameter and 150 feet in height. There are, however, some parts of some townships that have not restocked naturally and now the Forest Service is restocking some of those areas by artificial means of reproduction, especially in the Hebo country where planting on a large scale has been going on for more than five years.

***Siuslaw National Forest Land Classification Atlas*, 1919**

During the 1930s, the Civilian Conservation Corps crews planted trees in burned areas and logged-over land that had come into the Forest through New Deal land programs. This work increased later in the CCC years, as more lands came under National Forest management. By 1940, CCC Company 5436 at Camp Nestucca had planted 980 acres. In the late 1930s crews from the Resettlement Administration camps performed some tree planting, and after 1941 Conscientious Objectors reforested the Yachats Purchase Unit. During the 1950s high school students planted trees for fund raising events and for Arbor Day observations.

Planting crew, Mt. Hebo. C.P. Cronk photo, 1910-1911.

Planting crew and camp. C.P. Cronk photo, 1910-1911.

The planting of 200,000 Douglas fir seedlings was completed November 19. The work was started on October 29 by a planting crew from the Nestucca CCC camp. This planting is a continuation of the planting begun on the Kay Burn in 1910. The total plantation now covers an area of approximately 10,000 acres.

***Six Twenty-Six*, December 1935**

In later years, during maximum timber production, tree planting in the wake of timber sales became a major undertaking. In 1962, for example, crews planted 2,651,000 conifer seedlings on 4,237 acres of timber sales. Another 188 acres of steep hills were seeded by helicopter.[2] In the 1970s the contract planting crews developed a distinctive sub-culture. Many of these people were itinerant tree planters called "hoedads," who traveled throughout the Western states in dilapidated vehicles, wearing colorful attire.

Applying fertilizer with helicopter, 1950s.

Hoedad planting seedlings.

Seedling trees for reforestation in the 1960s came from the Forest nursery at Beaver Creek. This facility was dedicated to growing trees from seed and propagating trees from grafted stock. Fir and western hemlock cones were delivered to the nursery, seeds cleaned and planted, then the seedlings were transferred to storage at each District.

Don Oliver examining seedling, Beaver Creek Seed Nursery, 1960s.

Seedlings in greenhouse, Beaver Creek Seed Nursery, 1960s.

In 1935, the Camp Hebo CCC men participated in an experimental program of pruning 20-year old Douglas fir trees from the 1913 plantation. The trees had reached heights of 20 to 50 feet and a diameter of ten inches. The 1935 pruning program removed lower branches from selected trees to a height of 16 to 18 feet. By 1940, the Camp Nestucca group had pruned selected trees on 356 acres of fir plantations.[3] The goal of pruning the immature trees was to remove branches so that the trees would produce more clear lumber. The practice of pruning was briefly revived in recent years.

In addition to replanting the coniferous forests, the Siuslaw also undertook a planting program in the sand dunes along the coast between the mouth of the Siuslaw River and Coos Bay. This area was especially problematic for forestry because the shifting sand dunes did not lend themselves to tree culture. Pine trees do grow on sheltered areas where the sand is stabilized. The species of pine growing in the dunes is shore pine or *Pinus contorta*, which is widely distributed throughout the West, and is not generally considered a merchantable species. It is, however, successful in the dunes. Another introduced species, Monterey pine, proved vulnerable to disease.

Willow planting on the Dunes. C.P. Cronk photo, 1910-1911.

Planting Holland grass on the Dunes, ca. 1936.

Another type of planting peculiar to the Siuslaw is that of Holland grass for the purpose of preventing wind erosion of sand. This destructive agency has encroached on timber, clogged the outlets of steams, and destroyed recreation sites. Plantings of Holland grass aggregate 300 acres [each year].

A History of the Siuslaw National Forest, Oregon, as of December 31, 1939

As the program developed to plant the dunes, it had three phases. The first was to plant willow or European beach grass, which could stabilize the dunes and keep the sand in place. After the beach grass, crews propagated Scotch broom, which fixed nitrogen in the sand. Finally, pine trees could be planted with some hope of success. In 1959, for example, the Forest stabilized 463 acres of dunes, planting European beach grass on 126 acres, other grasses on 168 acres, Scotch broom on 25 acres, and shore pine on 55 acres, for a total cost of $47,000.[4]

Unfortunately, the European beach grass and the Scotch broom spread well beyond their intended space on the dunes. European beach grass covered so much of the dunes that it interfered with the nesting areas of the western snowy plover. Currently, the Siuslaw and the Oregon National Guard are cooperating in a beach grass eradication program. Scotch broom, another exogenous plant, has become an invasive species.

OTHER COMMERCIAL TREES

Homesteader Tom Agee carrying cascara bark.

Douglas fir, Sitka spruce, and western red cedar were by far the most important products on the Forest, but several other plants figure into the Siuslaw's history. The bark of the cascara tree is used as a laxative, and a lively trade in cascara bark developed before the turn of the century. Charles H. Flory wrote an Inspection Report on the cascara trade for the Forest in 1909. By that time the business of gathering the bark, drying it, and selling it to processors had passed the peak it reached in the 1890s. Flory's report is a remarkable source of information about this little-known botanical product.

Cascara grew in the coastal forests as isolated trees and shrubs with a diameter of up to eight inches. Cascara gatherers removed the bark from the lower trunk of the tree, then felled the tree so that they could remove the rest of the bark. The bark from a large tree could weigh as much as 100 pounds when green. Green bark had to be dried before it could be sold. The harvesting process destroyed the trees, of course, but the small trees were not cut, so there was a continuous supply of the product. Flory estimates that a man could produce about 100 pounds of dried bark each day. The price of the dried bark in the 1890s was 14 to 20 cents per pound. In 1909 the price had fallen to 4 to 5 cents per pound.

Inspecting dried bark at shipping point.

Flory points out that the cascara—or "chittim," as he calls it—was one of the few cash crops available to early settlers. "There is many a farmer in the coast mountains who owes his ability to have lived continuously on his place and improved it to the sale of chittim bark in the early days."[5] With the price falling and the demand diminishing in 1909, Flory recommended that the Forest not sell any cascara. In 1914, however, the Siuslaw made its first cascara sale as World War I increased the international demand. Within a few years, the price reached as high as 30 cents per pound for dried bark. The price declined through the 1920s and the market eventually collapsed. From 1914-1920 total cascara sales on the Forest amounted to 188 tons.[6]

Activity in the marketing of alder...began in 1928 when Ted Hornschuck cut in trespass on Pollard Creek and was made a sale for 330,000 board feet. For the next ten years he moved his small portable mill from place to place. In 1937 the demand for alder furniture stock increased sharply. Permanent alder mills were built in Beaver and Tillamook, and the Three Rivers Alder Company who operate the latter purchased in 1937 a tract of 4,100,000 board feet of alder on Beaver Creek.

A History of the Siuslaw National Forest, Oregon, as of December 31, 1939

A second deciduous tree that has had an interesting history is the red alder. Although this species was never a major part of the coastal lumber economy, it was the only western hardwood cut on a commercial scale on the national forests of Oregon.

Other commercial products from the Forest include greenery such as fern, salal, and huckleberry brush. Medicinal products include foxglove (digitalis), the root of Oregon grape, and yew.

A good crop of huckleberries.

Early commentators on the Siuslaw typically noted evidence of large fires that left snags and second growth over much of the area now included in the Forest. This fire episode is dated in the 1840s and is interpreted as either a single fire that covered perhaps 5,000 square miles, or a series of large (>200,000 acre) fires occurring from the 1840s until 1868.[7] Since there were people in the Coast Range who have left written accounts from these years without mentioning a 5,000 square mile fire, a succession of several fires during the 1840s seems a more likely explanation.

MAJOR NINETEENTH CENTURY SIUSLAW NF FIRES

FIRE	DATE	ESTIMATED SIZE	DISTRICTS AFFECTED
Umpqua	1840	450,000 acres	Mapleton Waldport
Nestucca	1853	320,000 acres	Hebo
Coos	1868	300,000 acres	Smith River
Yaquina Bay	1868	Unknown	Waldport

Source: *A History of the Siuslaw National Forest, Oregon, as of December 31, 1939*

Sometime in the 1840s a large and very destructive forest fire swept over the Coast Range, leaving in its wake for a stretch of about 150 miles in length and 30 to 40 miles in width, fire-killed timber, innumerable snags of which are still standing as grim witnesses of this great destruction. About 75 percent of the timber was completely destroyed, and huge trees from four to ten feet in diameter and over 200 feet in height were killed.

***Siuslaw National Forest Lands Classification Atlas*, 1919**

Although the Coast Range has ample rain in most months, it can be dry in the summer or fall and is highly subject to fire during those dry times. Records of the fires in 1910 and in the 1930s show that the coastal forest was very flammable when conditions were dry enough. Indeed the first European writer to comment on the Oregon coast may have seen evidence of a forest fire. Reverend Fletcher accompanied Sir Francis Drake on his circumnavigation in 1577-1578. During June 3-17, Drake's party visited the coast of "New Albion," generally supposed to have been Oregon. Fletcher complained of the cold and storms, the "vile, thicke and stinking fogges," and the "trees without leaves and the ground without greenes" in June and July.[8]

Remarks about forest fires from casual visitors are difficult to interpret because they had no way to gauge the size of a particular fire. The General Land Office survey teams were better able to measure the extent of the burned area. Surveys made in the 1872 to 1880 period note that three whole townships in the Hebo Ranger District had been completely burned by fires in the past. These were T 3 S, R 9 W and 10 W and

T 4 S, R 7 W. Further south, T 12 S, R 8 W, in the upper Big Elk Creek drainage immediately west of Marys Peak, was also described as completely burned by past fires.

Significant fire years on the central Oregon coast are 1840, 1849, 1853, and 1868. Three of these years—1840, 1849, and 1868—brought fires to other parts of western Oregon, including the lower Columbia, the Willamette Valley, and the Coos-Coquille area. In all probability, then, these were dry years in which most of western Oregon's forests were vulnerable.

The cause of Coast Range fires in the nineteenth century is open to question. The Coast Range is relatively free of summer lightning strikes. Since "dry"

EARLY SIUSLAW NF FIRES BY DRAINAGE

RIVER/ DRAINAGE	RANGER DISTRICT (HISTORIC)	FIRE YEAR	FIRE YEAR
Tillamook	Hebo	1868	1902
Nestucca	Hebo	1849	1868
Three Rivers	Hebo	1849	1868
Salmon	Hebo	1826	1849
Siletz		1840	1849
Yaquina		1849	1868
Alsea	Waldport	1849	1868
Yachats	Waldport	1849	1936
Siuslaw	Mapleton	1849	1868
Siltcoos	Smith River	1849	1868
Smith	Smith River	1840	1849
Umpqua	Smith River	1770	1826

Source: Zybach, "Great Fires of the Oregon Coast Range 1770-1933"

TOWNSHIPS REPORTED AS BURNED, GLO 1872

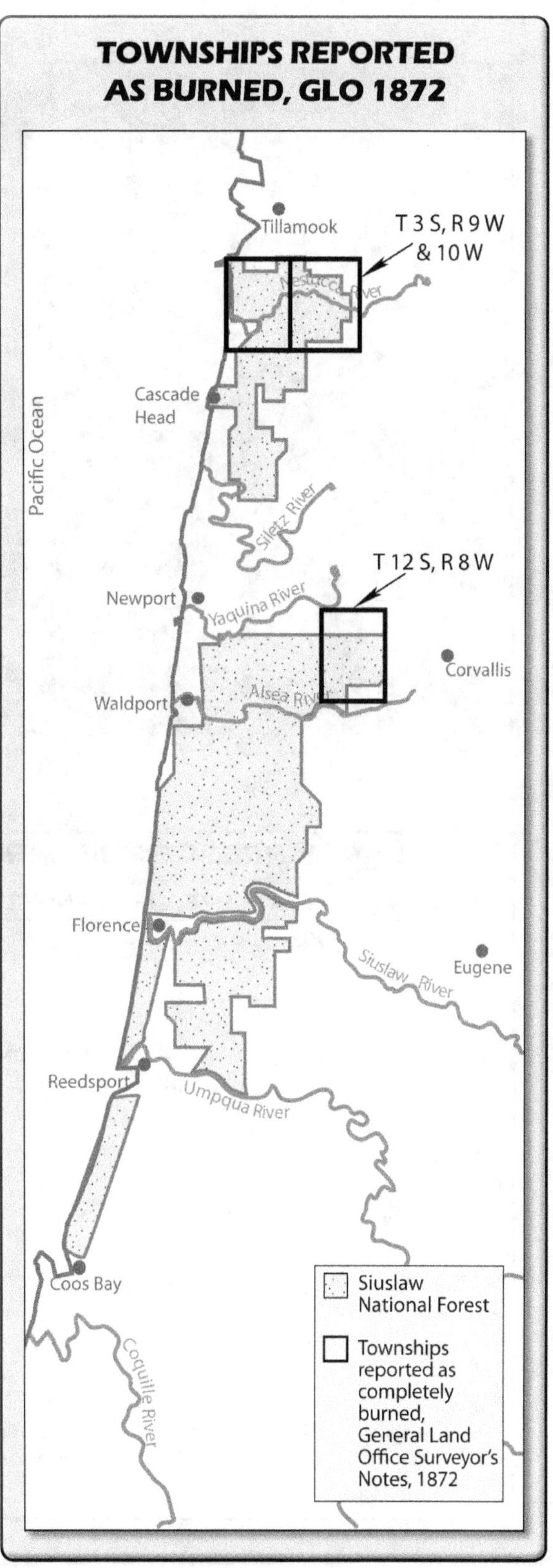

Mt. Hebo burn in light snow. C.P. Cronk photo, 1910-1911.

LARGE FIRES OF THE EARLY TWENTIETH CENTURY				
FIRE NAME	**YEAR**	**SIZE** (ACRES)	**RANGER DISTRICT**	**NOTES**
1902 fires	1902			The Yacolt Fire in SW Washington and NW Oregon burned over one million acres. Recorded only as a bad fire year on the coast
1910 fires	1910		Hebo, others	Multiple fires throughout the Forest
Triangle Lake, others	1929	14,000	Mapleton	
Tillamook Burn	1933	267,000		Best known fire in Oregon history, did not reach the Siuslaw
Big Creek or Yachats	1936	10,000		Burned on Blodgett Tract within the Siuslaw
Smith River, others	1938	11,500	Smith River	
Second Tillamook Burn	1939	1,700	Hebo	Re-burned much of the 1933 burn and spread to 1,700 acres on the Siuslaw
1951 fires	1951	1,599	35 small fires throughout the Forest	He-He Fire and Detroit Fire on the Willamette NF and Vincent Creek on Coos Bay District, BLM

North Lake after 1910 burn, Mt. Hebo. C.P. Cronk photo, 1910-1911.

lightning accounts for most natural fires, fires on the coast are generally attributable to human causes. The 1840-1868 period of great burns was also a period of increased Euro-American entry into the coast country. Native groups in the Willamette Valley had burned grasslands each fall for generations, but this practice was not known to be widespread in the Coast Range. Euro-Americans, on the other hand, used fires for clearing land of brush, ferns, and even trees. While we do not know the origin of the earliest recorded fires, most the fires in the years after 1908 began as clearing fires that got away from land owners adjacent to the Forest.

Valsetz fire, 1953, east of the Siuslaw.

We have had several bad fires in the 21 years I have been in the coast country, but in nearly all cases they started on lands outside our protective unit and were large fires by the time they reached our boundaries.

Ranger Edward S. Kerby, 1945

FIRE CONTROL

With the formation of the Forest Reserves and the National Forest, fire control and fire prevention became a political issue. Prior to 1908, fires on public land were not considered especially important, as long as they were not perceived to be dangerous. Settlers considered burning brush and ferns for clearing as their right. Early Forest Service personnel needed to convince people that wildfires resulting from clearing or annual light burning wasted important public resources. In the years immediately following the formation of the Forest, local residents who opposed Forest Service management expressed their opposition by deliberately setting fires. Incendiarism did not last long on the Siuslaw, but it was a factor in early management.

The bell wether leading the opposition against the Forest Service at the time was Lorenzo E. Doel. He was wholly unscrupulous and would stop at nothing to gain his ends. ...About 1920 we convicted him in federal court of setting fire on the public domain. This was the last of Mr. Doel as far as we were concerned.

Ranger Edward S. Kerby, 1945

Fire control in the early period was hazardous and often frustrating. Fires in remote areas were difficult to detect and difficult to reach. Fire crews were hired from the local "labor pool," and they seldom had experience in fire fighting. Fire lines were made by hand through the brush and ferns. Supplies, communication, and payments for the crews were hard for the Forest Service to arrange.

The fires of 1910 were widespread on the Siuslaw and throughout the West, especially in the Rocky Mountains. Partly as a result of the 1910 experiences, the Forest Service focused efforts on fire prevention, detection, and suppression. After World War I, the Forest Service contracted with the Army Air Corps to provide planes to find fires during critical months. A network of Forest Service lookouts was built after 1910. The Civilian Conservation Corps built numerous lookouts during the 1930s.

Lookouts Guarding the Siuslaw

LOOKOUTS

Buzzard Butte
South Point
Bell Mountain
Mt. Hebo
Little Hebo
Cougar Mountain
Gauldy Mountain
Niagra Point
Square Top
Hilltop
Cape Mountain
Table Mountain
Grass Mountain

Marys Peak lookout, built by the CCC.

Early platform style.

Alsea Ridge (State)
Pioneer Butte
Prairie Peak
Cummins Peak
Herman Peak
Cannibal Mountain
Marys Peak
Siltcoos
Fern Top (State)
Roman Nose (BLM)
Goodwin Peak
Divide
Henderson Peak
Windy Peak

Later cupola style.

View from Square Top Lookout, 1937.

In mid August of 1910 Ranger Russell and I counted 16 fires burning at one time. During the worst six weeks, I have a recollection of not sleeping in my bed more than once or twice. Most of the time we had less than a dozen men and could only peck away at where the danger seemed greatest. At the last blow-up we were working on a fire on top of Mt. Hebo in the old burn. We got that corralled, or thought so. When we saw smoke near Dolph, heading for Cloverdale, we started for that. When we had gone only a few miles, we saw the Hebo fire breaking out again. Russell sent me back with my blanket, tarp, shovel, mattock, and ax to get some men from Hebo for a new attack. I started back with 60 pounds of grub thinking that I alone at night might be able to hold the fire. I did manage to hold quite a length of fire line, but in the morning the wind rose and I found myself with a nice fire line but with the fire going around me on both sides. I should probably have headed for a small pond but I was thinking more of making the ridge trail. Fortunately, I did know the country. With the increased wind velocity the fire was advancing more rapidly through the tops of the snags than on the ground. I figured I had a chance to make the trail before the fire crossed it. My one thought was to beat the fire down the mountain.

C.P. Cronk, 1910-1911

The biggest job we had was to convince the [Euro-American] natives that the light burning in the spring and fall of open fern and salal patches was inimical to the cause of forestry and accomplished nothing but to kill the young trees and perpetuate the bracken fern which is entirely useless. The thing that made it so difficult was that perfectly sincere and otherwise law-abiding citizens would burn fern on their own lands and frequently allow it to spread to other lands. They contended, and they were right in their contentions, that these early spring and fall fern fires would only run through the opening and stop when they reached the green timber. The very small trees which rarely had the opportunity to get their heads above the fern were not seen by those doing the burning.

Ranger Edward S. Kerby, 1945

Slide on Canal Creek.

Because of its position on the coast, the Siuslaw is vulnerable to large Pacific storms which cause extensive damage. The most severe of these within recent history was the Columbus Day Storm of October 12, 1962. Other notable storms on the coast occurred on January 9, 1880, in 1948, in 1995, and in December, 2007. The Columbus Day Storm was significant for the intensity of its wind and the damage it caused, but also for the sheer size of the area involved. The storm cut a swath through the West Coast from Eureka, California, to southern British Columbia. The path of the storm was about 1,000 miles long and 125 miles wide, engaging the Coast Range, southwestern Oregon, the Willamette Valley, the lower Columbia, southwestern Washington, Puget Sound, and southern British Columbia. Wind velocity was difficult to measure because the anemometers at exposed points were either damaged or reached the maximum on their scale. The radar station at Hebo, for example, registered only to 135 MPH, but the winds were estimated at 170 MPH. The weather station in Corvallis measured a gust of 127 MPH immediately before it was destroyed. At Cape Blanco, gusts reached 145 MPH; at Vancouver BC, wind was measured at over 58 MPH. The wind caused damage as far inland as Spokane.

Damage to Camp Cleawox, 1962.

Meterologists recognized the storm as an extra-tropical cyclone and estimated that the actual center was 40 miles off shore. Barometric pressure was extremely low—28.6 inches of mercury. Other storms have caused substantial damage to the Forest, but the Columbus Day Storm was by far the strongest and most extensive.

The storm passed through the most populous areas of

Forest roads were blocked by blow-downs.

Oregon and Washington, and through the heavily forested areas of the California Redwoods, the Coast Range, the west slope of the Cascades, and the Olympic Range. The damage to timber in Oregon was estimated at six billion board feet and in Washington at five billion board feet. Trees blown down in the forest damaged other trees, and trees near habitation damaged power lines, destroyed buildings, crushed cars, and blocked roads. All national forests west of the Cascades in Oregon were affected.

Estimates for wind-downed timber on the Siuslaw reached 740 million board feet within a few days of the storm.[9] The annual cut at this time was around 350 million, so the storm damage equaled more than two years' sales. The Forest held salvage sales as quickly as possible and extended existing sales contracts so that loggers could cut the downed timber before it lost value. All downed timber was to be removed by May 1, 1964. Eighteen foresters from other national forests were detailed to the Siuslaw to organize the salvage sales.

Salvage logging efforts continued into the mid-1960s.

In addition to the timber damage, the Forest had to deal with extensive damage to infrastructure. Telephone and power lines were lost. Campgrounds were damaged. Over 1,000 miles of forest roads had to be cleared for use.

Storm damage included flooding on the Nestucca River.

After the Columbus Day Storm, the next weather problem occurred when the Meadow Lake dam west of Carlton broke on November 20. The resultant flood of the Nestucca smashed the Nestucca River Bridge, which cost $30,000 to replace. Over $500 damage was done to the Rocky Bend Campground.

Siuslaw National Forest Historical Notes for 1962

Damage to campgrounds occurred throughout the Forest.

NOTES

1 Data from *Siuslaw National Forest Land Classification Atlas* (on file, Waldport, OR: Siuslaw NF, 1919) 3.

2 "Historical Notes for 1962" (on file, Waldport, OR: Siuslaw NF, 1963).

3 *Six Twenty-Six,* December 1935, 19; *Coast Range Beacon,* April 1940, 2.

4 "Historical Notes for 1959" (on file, Waldport, OR: Siuslaw NF, 1960).

5 Charles H. Flory, "The Chittim Bark Industry" (on file, Waldport, OR: Siuslaw NF, 1909) 6.

6 *A History of the Siuslaw National Forest, Oregon, as of December 31, 1939* (on file, Waldport, OR: Siuslaw NF, 1939) 41.

7 See Bob Zybach, "The Great Fires of the Oregon Coast Range: 1770-1933" (on file, Corvallis, OR: Siuslaw NF, 1988), for an ambitious (though incomplete in this version) chronicle of post-contact fires, as recorded by contemporary observers.

8 Zybach, 62. Reverend Fletcher quoted in Charles Carey, *General History of Oregon* (Portland, OR: OHS, 1971) 37.

9 "Historical Notes for 1962" (on file, Waldport, OR: Siuslaw NF, 1963) discusses the storm and its aftermath.

CHAPTER FOUR

THE SIUSLAW AND THE WORLD WARS

WORLD WAR I

The Siuslaw National Forest occupies a comfortable location on Oregon's coast, remote by some standards, and usually considered far enough from the events of the outside world to provide tranquility. During the great wars of the twentieth century, however, the people of the Siuslaw found themselves caught up in the events occurring half a world away, in Europe and Asia.

During World War I the Sitka spruce timber on the Siuslaw became a strategic material for making military aircraft. During World War II, the Siuslaw and the Oregon coast in general found itself exposed on the western fringe of the continent, closest to Japan's imperial ambitions. In 1942 the Japanese military invaded and occupied some of the Aleutian islands in Alaska. In Oregon, they shelled Fort Stevens, bombed the coast near Brookings, and sent balloon bombs which killed six people near Bly. Civilians on the coast served as aircraft observers, formed citizen militias, and blacked out all lights at night. During the Cold War, the radar stations at Mt. Hebo scanned the skies for enemy aircraft.

HERE COMES THE KNOCKOUT!
A Cartoon by R. H. Browning, Forest Guard

WORLD WAR I — AIRCRAFT FOR THE WAR AND SPRUCE FOR AIRCRAFT

World War I began in Europe in 1914. By 1916 both the Allies and the Axis were bogged down in trench warfare in which neither side could gain an advantage. The U.S. entered the war early in 1917 convinced that bringing fresh troops and the additional industrial capacity would help the Allies prevail in the "stalemate in the trenches." This was true, but the situation was complicated by several factors. The U.S. military needed time to mobilize, and American industries were not producing the right products for the war.

One of these products was aircraft, which was recognized as a technological solution to trench warfare. Aircraft could fly over the lines, bomb the enemy, and return to base. Military aircraft were made of lumber and silk. The lumber needed to be flawless, light, and strong. The best material was Sitka spruce, which was available only in the coastal forests of Oregon, Washington, British Columbia, and Alaska. During the winter of 1916-1917, the European aircraft manufacturers discovered Sitka spruce and placed large orders with west coast lumber companies. Prices for Sitka spruce rose, and supplies went down. When the U.S. entered the war, there was very little Sitka spruce lumber available.[1]

> **Spruce is really a by-product of our other woods, and can as a rule only be produced as it comes in with cedar, fir, or western hemlock. There are some small tracts of timber along the coast where spruce predominates. The greater proportion of the spruce on these lowland tracts is of inferior quality, so that only a very small percentage of upper grades [of lumber] is produced from it. Growing in with this spruce is a very inferior quality of cedar and western hemlock which must be logged at the same time as the spruce. By the time the logger or mill man disposes of the low grade cedar and western hemlock ... and 50 percent of the spruce for box lumber, he begins to realize that he needs a very fancy price for the shop lumber and aeroplane stock which remains.**
>
> **Ralph Burnside, Willapa Lumber Co, Willapa, Washington, in *The Timberman*, January 1917**

The U.S. Army created the Aircraft Production Board and the War Emergency Spruce Council. They ordered 100 million board feet of clear spruce lumber to be delivered during the fall of 1917. The American aircraft manufacturers could not use this amount of spruce since they were not yet capable of producing aircraft on a wartime scale. Throughout the war, 70 percent of the spruce went to aircraft factories in Europe.

Oregon and Washington lumber companies were eager to fill the order. Labor organizations were quick to see that the war presented an opportunity to strike for better working conditions. As the West Coast lumber industry prepared to meet the wartime

Willamette Iron and Steel ad in The Timberman.

> **At close range it appears that the powerful, unseen, foreign hand, which has directed this campaign of industrial unrest, is bent solely on the destruction of the social fabric. When the entire facts are known this country will be shaken to its very depths.**
>
> ***The Timberman*, July 1917**

order for spruce, the labor groups prepared for a conflict of their own. On March 5 and 6, 1917, the radical Industrial Workers of the World (IWW or Wobblies) organized the Lumber Workers Industrial Union in Spokane. They demanded better wages, improved camp conditions, and an 8-hour working day. The union set a strike date for July unless their demands were met. The shingle weavers' union in Seattle convened in May and made similar demands, with a July 16 strike date. The American Federation of Labor International Union of Timber Workers joined them. The stage was set for a major confrontation between the West Coast lumbermen and the workers, and on July 16, the strike began. By August 1, no more than 15 percent of the mills were running.[2] Total Sitka spruce production for the summer season of 1917 was 300 thousand board feet, rather than 100 million. The mill owners blamed the workers, and the workers blamed the owners.

I love my flag, I do, I do,
Which floats upon the breeze.
I also love my arms and legs,
And neck, and nose, and knees.
One little shell might spoil them all.
Or give them such a twist,
They wouldn't be of use to me;
I guess I won't enlist.

Wobbly (IWW) song quoted in Tyler, 1967

THE SPRUCE PRODUCTION DIVISION

Colonel Brice P. Disque.

As a result of the industry's failure to produce enough spruce for the war, General Pershing, U.S. Army Commanding General, appointed Colonel Brice P. Disque to create a "Spruce Production Division" (SPD) within the Army to supplement the recalcitrant West Coast loggers and mill workers. By January of 1918 Disque had created 34 squadrons of SPD soldiers to work in the logging camps and lumber mills. He developed plans for three new government mills, at Toledo, Oregon; Vancouver, Washington; and Port Angeles, Washington. He also created the Loyal Legion of Loggers and Lumbermen, a government-sponsored labor organization to neutralize the radical Wobblies and represent workers' goals to the mill owners.

Amazingly, the Spruce Production Division and Colonel Disque were successful. Folk humor records that Disque "came to see and stayed to saw." The result was one of the most unusual and controversial actions of the military during the war.

SPD troops at Toledo.

In its short life, the SPD provided Army labor in logging camps and lumber mills. It built and operated 13 logging railroads, purchased timber lands, and built three lumber mills of its own. The SPD mill at Toledo was a conventional sawmill, as was the mill at Port Angeles. The Vancouver mill was a re-manufacturing plant or, as the Army called it, a "cut-up" mill. The spruce logs were first cut at other mills into cants or large square timbers, and then they were shipped to Vancouver to be finished into airplane stock. Since aircraft spruce required rigid quality control, Disque felt that he would have the best success by doing his own final milling in an Army-run plant.

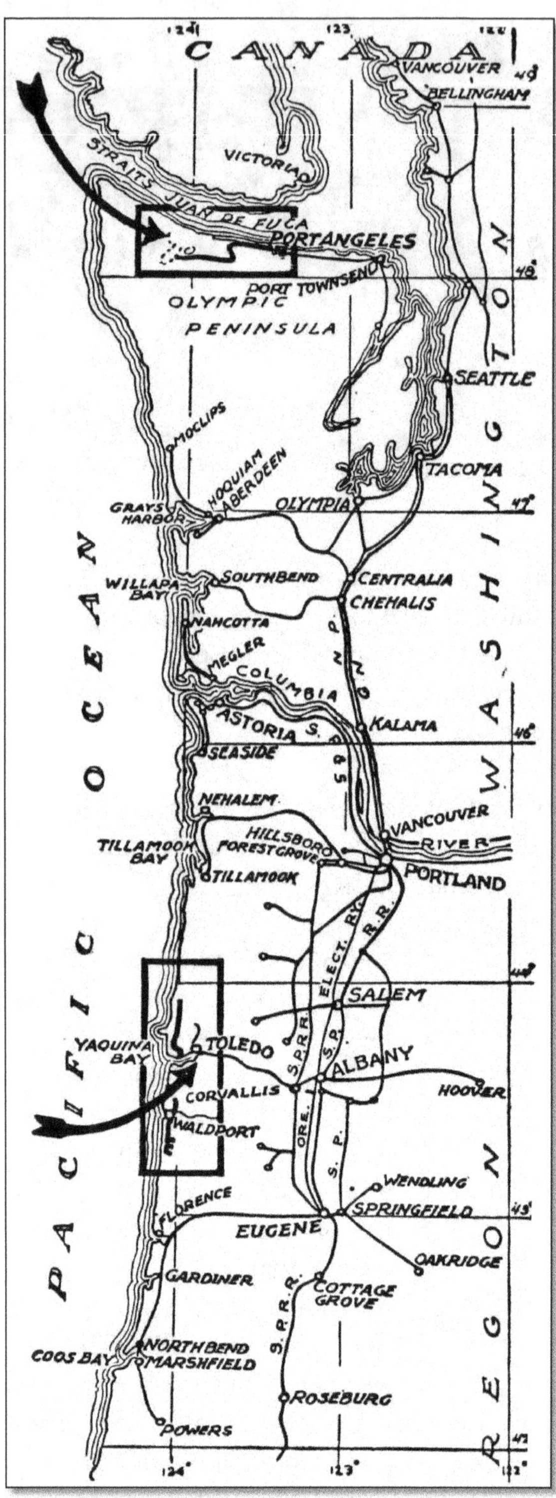

SPD projects at Toledo and Port Angeles.

The scale of the SPD operation was impressive. The SPD soldiers cut one million board feet of finished spruce aircraft stock per day at Vancouver, with a crew of 6,000 men working three shifts. The SPD divided the West Coast into six divisions—Puget Sound, Grays Harbor, Vancouver, Clatsop, Coos Bay, and Yaquina Bay—extending its influence into virtually all of the Northwest coast logging area. The strength of the Division grew to 27,685 men and 1,142 officers by May of 1918. By the end of the war six months later, it would surpass 30,000 men.

The Spruce Production Division was successful at producing aircraft quality spruce, but the demand for that product ended when the war ended and military aircraft of the next generation were not made of spruce. The legacy of the SPD was its success at solving the problems of labor-management relations in the lumber industry.

Visits to logging camps and mills convinced Colonel Disque that the IWW propaganda had not exaggerated the miserable living and working conditions that the loggers had to endure. Loggers lived in crowded camps without bathing facilities and with no provision for bedding or laundry. The food in some camps was inedible. "Disque was filled with sick dismay that American workers in the twentieth century had to live as the loggers did."[3]

Disque's policy was to make SPD soldiers available to work in the mills

Group photo taken at Toledo, 1918.

and camps, but the trade-off was that the lumber companies had to meet strict Army standards for hours, housing, and sanitation, and to pay a reasonable wage. "It is the present plan that troops should board with the logging company...if this cannot be done without crowding, a separate mess hall should be built for the troops." All troops were to receive "the same pay as civilian labor," and that pay was to be $3.50 per 8-hour day for loggers and less for common laborers. Pay was to be drawn every two weeks, and no charges were to be deducted for medical service. The document goes on to list specifications for "recreation rooms," "bathing facilities," "latrines," "sleeping facilities," and "dry rooms." These very issues—especially the pay scale, the 8-hour day, showers, and bedding—had been the crux of the IWW's campaign for the previous ten years. The mill owners became apoplectic, but they had to comply if they wanted to sell lumber to the government.

SPD camp, Toldeo. Canvas was a poor shelter in the coastal rain, 1918.

LLLL women working in a Coos Bay mill. *Timberman* photo.

LOYAL LEGION OF LOGGERS AND LUMBERMEN

MEMBERSHIP CARD

This is to Certify, That K K Robinson has become a Member of the **Loyal Legion of Loggers and Lumbermen** for the duration of the war by taking oath to devote his efforts to the production of Logs and Lumber for **Army Airplanes and Ships**, to be used against our common enemy, and to do every act and thing within his power to further the cause of the United States of America in the present conflict.

By authority of the Secretary of War. No. 59789

M. E. Crumpacker

1st Lieut. Signal Corps, U. S. Army, Officer in Charge

Dated this Sep 3" day of Sept 19[illegible]

LLLL membership card.

Loyal Legion of Loggers and Lumbermen Code

-To maintain the 8-hour day
-To ensure a "just and equitable wage"
-To standardize conditions in camps and mills
-To create a community spirit
-To encourage cooperative hospitals
-To provide health and accident insurance and pensions
-To institute employment service
-To further recreation and education
-To establish a common ground among labor and owners
-To promote better relationship within the industry
-To provide the means for amicable adjustment of issues
-To provide information within the industry
-To promote settlement of logged-over land
-To develop loyalty to the U.S.

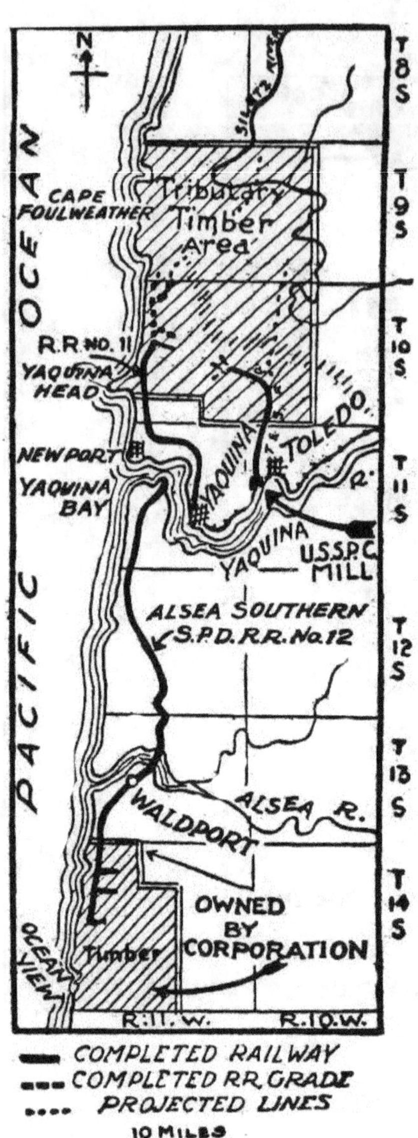

Timber lands accessed by SPD railroads from Toledo.

Yaquina Bay was one of the Spruce Production Division's best regions for obtaining old-growth Sitka spruce. Their plans for the area included a mill in Toledo and three new logging railroads. One railroad, designated Spruce Railroad X, would run north from Toledo to tap the spruce timber in the Siletz valley. This was an improvement of an existing railroad built by Toledo lumberman J.P. Miller.[4] The second railroad, Spruce Railroad XI, would run north along the coast to reach the spruce stands between Yaquina Bay and Cape Foulweather. The third, Spruce Railroad XII, would run south from Toledo and cross Alsea Bay to tap the spruce timber on a private tract owned by Michigan lumberman John W. Blodgett. This land was located between Waldport and Yachats and contained some of the best Sitka spruce timber in the U.S. Disque calculated that the Blodgett Tract could provide one million board feet of spruce each day until the estimated 300 to 500 million feet of spruce was exhausted.[5]

In January of 1918 Disque and the SPD obtained an option to buy spruce timber on the Blodgett Tract. In February the first squadrons of SPD soldiers arrived in Toledo and began work on the mill and the railroads.

Spruce Railroad XII, also called the Alsea Southern, was an ambitious railroad that compared to the Spruce Railroad I, built on the Olympic

SPD soldiers build Railroad XII, 1918.

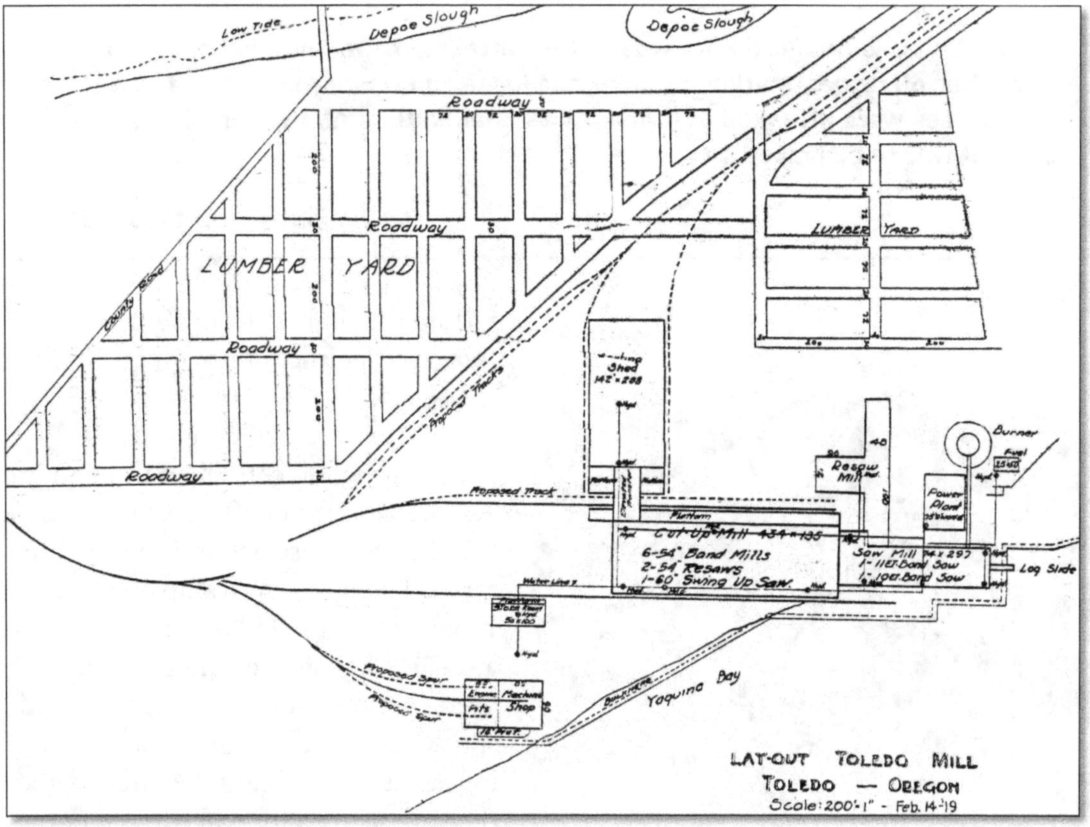

LAY-OUT TOLEDO MILL
TOLEDO — OREGON
Scale: 200'-1" - Feb. 14-'19

Plan of Toledo mill.

Peninsula in Washington. It ran south from Toledo requiring a trestle across Alsea Bay and sophisticated civil engineering to get through the coastal hills and over the numerous creeks along the route. Construction began in April of 1918 at South Beach on Yaquina Bay, where a new terminal and pier would become the booming grounds and the ferry port.

The Warren Spruce Company was the prime contractor for the new line. They built an average of two miles of railroad each day. The construction crew consisted of 4,200 soldiers and civilians working from 33 separate construction camps. Photographs taken by the Army show that the earthwork was done by horses and Fresno scrapers. Huge crews of soldiers laid the steel rails by hand. Bridge and trestle building preceded the railroad and required

Building Railroad XII, 1918.

Piling and large bridge timber was put in rafts and towed outside the [Yaquina] bar. When off its destination it was turned loose and washed ashore by the waves. Here horses were attached to it and it was snaked through the sand to the point where it was to be placed.

***The Timberman,* October 1918**

SPD at the Agate Beach Hotel, Newport.

rafting the timbers from Yaquina Bay, then sending them through the surf to the beach.

Construction continued through the summer and fall of 1918. On November 8, 1918, the construction crews had the railroad complete to Camp 1 on the Blodgett Tract. On November 11, the armistice was signed, and the war was over. Although the Army cut very little spruce from the Blodgett Tract before the armistice, building the railroad and the logging operation in seven months was a substantial achievement.

SPD Shay locomotive on Railroad XII.

The Blodgett Tract was a parcel totaling 12,700 acres of land south of Waldport and north of Yachats. It is now a part of the Siuslaw National Forest, having been incorporated into the Forest as the Yachats Purchase Unit in 1941. The tract had a remarkable history. It was wrested from the public domain by a fraudulent timber operator, then bought by the Army, then logged by a lumber company, then bought by the Siuslaw, and re-forested by conscientious objectors.

Mature Sitka spruce on the Blodgett Tract, ca. 1927.

John W. Blodgett bought the tract from C.A. Smith on May 31, 1917. Apparently, Smith was in default on some bonds Blodgett held, and the tract was in part compensation for the bonds. Blodgett's agent in Portland, P.S. Brunby, warned Blodgett that Smith was under indictment, and that some titles on his lands were being disallowed by the courts.[6]

Nevertheless, Blodgett completed the purchase. The SPD identified the tract as one of the best stands of Sitka spruce available. In January of 1918 the SPD contacted Brumby to arrange an option to buy the timber on the tract. The SPD began building the railroad south from Toledo to reach the tract in April of 1918, but negotiations for the timber were not complete. Blodgett was uncertain about selling the spruce on the tract without selling the fir as well. Disque and the SPD did not want the fir. Negotiations dragged on through the spring of 1918. The SPD was spending $30,000 per mile to build the railroad to the Blodgett Tract, but they had no assurance that they would be able to log the tract when they got the railroad finished.

By July Colonel Disque was fuming about Blodgett's intractable stand against selling the timber. On July 20, Disque sent a telegram to Blodgett threatening to commandeer the tract. The sale was finally settled in December of 1918 after the armistice had ended the war in November. The SPD paid Blodgett $635,000 for the tract. The deed recorded the acreage as 12,700 which brought the price to $50 per acre.

> **We must have permission to start operating in your timber commonly known as the Wright-Blodgett Tract south of Alsea Bay [stop] Will you agree to this entry with the understanding that if we cannot agree on price that the same will be legally commandeered [signed] Disque**
>
> **Disque to Blodgett, Blodgett Papers, July 20, 1918**

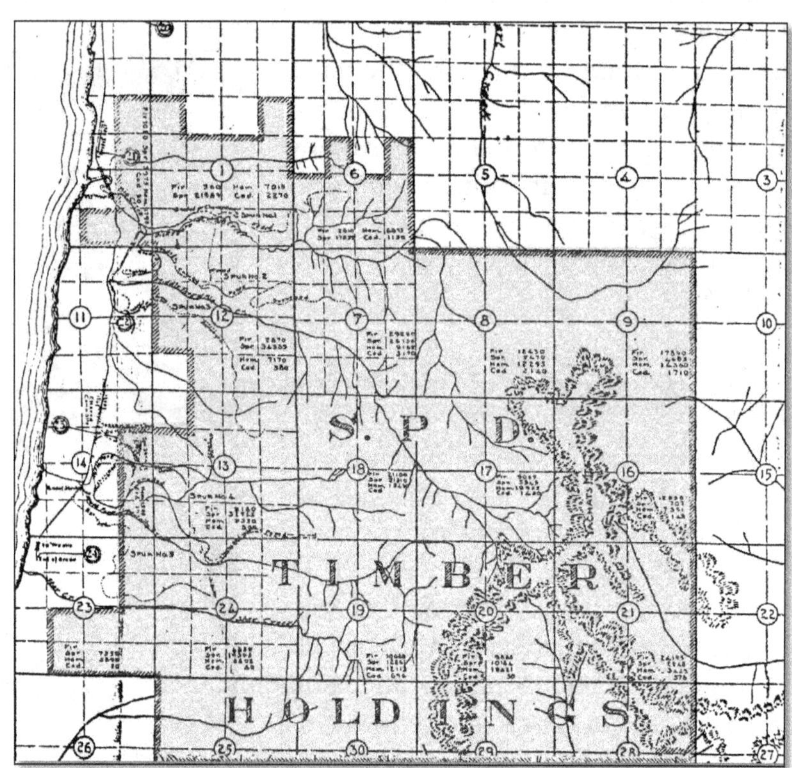

SPD map of the Blodgett Tract.

After the war, the Army held a sale of all the SPD assets, including the mills at Toledo, Vancouver, and Port Angeles, timber lands, railroads, logging equipment, and even a hotel the SPD had bought in Port Angeles. The Blodgett Tract timber inventoried at 300 million board feet of Douglas fir, 250 million board feet of spruce, 200 million feet of western hemlock, and 15 million feet of cedar.[7] The mill at Toledo, the Railroad, and the Blodgett Tract languished on the auction block for several months until a group of investors agreed to purchase the package for $2,000,000 in December of 1920. They formed Pacific Spruce Corporation. The government's terms were very favorable, asking only $50,000 down on the properties, and carrying the sales contract for 10 years.[8]

SPRUCE PRODUCTION DIVISION SOLDIERS IN LINCOLN COUNTY

Health Problems

Hernia	8
Heart problem	6
Varicose veins	5
Rheumatism	4
Mental deficiency	2
Flat feet	2
Leg injury	2
Tuberculosis	2
Old injuries	2
Arm or elbow	1
Appendicitis	1
Bullet wound	1
Asthma	1
Lead poisoning	1
Indigestion	1
Bright's disease	1
Undiagnosed	2

Yaquina District SPD, Weekly Medical Reports, August 27, 1918

Spruce soldiers assigned to operations in Lincoln County were mostly employed in construction of the Toledo mill and the railroads. Some worked as loggers in the Siletz valley with the Warren Spruce Company. Contemporary photos show them living in squad tents, eating in mess halls, and visiting Newport when they were off duty.

One Spruce soldier has left a lively account of his experiences in the SPD in Toledo and Waldport. This was Floyd R. Marsh, who enlisted in the Army in Colorado and was trained as a pharmacy technician. He found himself assigned to the newly-formed SPD.

> *"If it had not been the Major telling me this, I would have thought it was some kind of a joke. I had never heard of the Spruce Division."*[9]

Marsh found the Spruce soldiers busy in the spring of 1918.

> *The Spruce Division worked fast in the few days it took us to go to Waldport and set up our infirmary tent. They had started a sawmill, laid a track for a logging train and were logging. The government built railroads right into the forest to get the spruce out.*[10]

Soldiers crowd Newport waterfront.

By the fall of 1918, the troops' energy had diminished:

> *"The camp was a little tent city, and like the last days at Waldport, it was full of men playing cards, rolling dice, and just plain loafing."*[11]

On November 11, 1918, the armistice ended the war in Europe. The war in Lincoln County dragged on for a few more months as Spruce Production Corps troops and equipment left the area for Vancouver Barracks. There, the troops were mustered out of the Army, and the logging and railroad equipment was assembled for the final auction sale held the following year.

WORLD WAR II — THE WAR ON THE SIUSLAW

After the U.S. entered World War II in 1941, several changes affected the Forest Service and the Siuslaw National Forest. The first of these was a vigorous war market for timber. Between 1930 and 1939, during the Depression, the Siuslaw sold 22 million board feet of timber. During the war years, 1941-1946, the Forest sold 188 million board feet.

During the Depression, the Forest Service was adequately staffed, and the Civilian Conservation Corps was able to provide reserve manpower for fire fighting, road building, and maintenance work. When the U.S. entered World War II, 2,000 Forest Service staff nationwide joined the armed forces. Throughout the war, draft and enlistment reduced the Forest Service to the point that personnel for sale management, maintenance, and fire fighting were stretched thin.

The Forest Service put out a call for volunteers, and public-spirited Oregonians staffed lookouts and performed other duties on a volunteer basis. Thirty-two lookouts on the Mt. Hood National Forest and one on the Siuslaw were staffed with volunteers, who were called the Forest Service Reserve.[12]

Additional staffing of lookouts was done by the Aircraft Warning Service (AWS) during the war. This organization began in the late 1930s, and became active in 1941 as part of the

Observer station overlooking the Salmon River estuary.

Civilian Defense effort. AWS observers, also called the Ground Observer Corps, were civilians who volunteered their time to watch for enemy aircraft. Numbers of observers on the west Coast have been estimated at about 150,000.[13] In general, AWS lookouts in and adjacent to the Hebo Ranger District reported to the Portland Filter Center. These included Buzzard Butte, Bell Mountain, Mt. Hebo, Little Hebo, and Cougar Mountain. Those south of Hebo on and adjacent to the Siuslaw National Forest reported to the Eugene Filter Center. These lookouts included Cape Mountain, Prairie Peak, Cummins Peak, Cannibal Mountain, Siltcoos, Fern Top (Oregon State Forestry), Roman Nose (BLM), Goodwin Peak, Henderson Peak, and Windy Peak.[14] For firefighting, the Forest Service had access to trained crews from Oregon's three Civilian Public Service (CPS) camps, at Waldport on the Siuslaw, Cascade Locks on Mt. Hood, and Elkton on the Umpqua. The CPS also staffed lookouts.

Logging companies also felt the same shortage of experienced manpower. For the first two years of the war, logging was not a draft-exempt employment, so loggers who did not enlist could be drafted. Worse, many older more experienced loggers moved to shipyard jobs in Portland, which were considerably more remunerative than logging, and were draft-exempt. In the spring of 1943, the Selective Service Commission granted occupational deferments to loggers, and the situation improved. Most historians agree, however, that as a result of sparse crews and inexperienced men, the war-time industry moved towards new less physically demanding technology. This included diesel tractors, gasoline-powered chain saws, and motor trucks. The days of railroad logging, steam-powered yarders, and crosscut saws were numbered.

Rex [Wakefield, Forest Supervisor] tried to enlist, and they said they needed him more in the Forest than they did in the military. Some of his buddies tried to enlist. They said. "If you're doing anything at all, stay there, because we're just spinning our wheels here."

Mabel Wakefield Interview, 1989

THE WAR ON THE COAST

The Siuslaw's strategic position on the Oregon coast created extra pressure during the early years of the war. By 1941 the Japanese military had perfected a strategy of amphibious assault in its rapid advance across the Pacific. The strategy of "island hopping" had brought the Japanese occupation forces to the Pacific islands, southeast Asia, New Guinea, and Alaska. Coastal areas like Lincoln and Lane counties were perceived as especially vulnerable because of their relative isolation. Highway 101 and the major bridges were in place, providing a route for vehicles along the coast. The Coast Range was very thinly populated, however, and access from the Willamette Valley to the coast was limited to a few roads.

The military and the civilians were nervous. Japanese-Americans were removed from their homes in Oregon, Washington, and California lest they become a "fifth column" supporting invading forces, as German civilians had in northern Europe. The Japanese shelling of Fort Stevens and the bombing of Brookings in 1942 were other concrete events that ratcheted up the level of tension. The military responded by instituting civil defense programs, conducting increased surveillance by air and sea, supporting local militias, and stationing troops to patrol the beaches on horseback and on foot with dogs. For most Americans this level of defense would have seemed excessive or even paranoid, but people on the coast felt exposed, and public preparedness was no doubt reassuring.

Above: Soldiers on mounted patrol. Left: Dog patrol at Heceta Head lightstation

I was a dog trainer here [Heceta Head lightstation] during World War II. The dogs were used for beach patrol. One time the country had submarine alerts, so the Coast Guard had beach patrol dogs. We patrolled the beaches from the hill by Sea Lion Caves, where it's close to the beach then north to Yachats.

William Dean McCord Interview, 1997

Blimps patrolled the coast. LCHS photo.

Blimp off Cape Foulweather.

The military conducted coastal patrols by blimps which were based in hangars located at Tillamook. These slow-moving aircraft flew at low altitudes over the beaches. Civilian boats performed offshore patrol duties. The *Kingfisher*, a well-known charter boat based in Depoe Bay, was outfitted for patrol service and painted grey to reduce her visibility. Now, over 65 years later, the *Kingfisher* is still in commission and one of the few Oregon vessels listed in the National Register of Historic Places. Army and Coast Guard personnel were stationed at lookout structures located at good viewpoints along the coast, like Cascade Head.

The *Kingfisher* in military service. LCHS photo.

For people living near the coast, blackouts of all lights including automobile lights, were required. Failure to observe the blackout resulted in arrest and fine. By November of 1942, 64 people had been arrested in Lincoln County for blackout violations. In one instance, two young men were arrested, but later released to the custody of a Navy recruiting officer. They had agreed to enlist.[15]

As soon as it turned dark you had black shades that you pulled over your windows. And you had a piece of material that went over the headlights of your car, and if you did any driving you could hardly see two or three feet ahead of your car.

Mabel Wakefield Interview, 1989

Men and women volunteered for the AWS, which stationed observers along the coast to watch for enemy aircraft. Men in Lincoln County volunteered for the Beach Patrol, a local militia armed with hunting rifles. They drilled on the weekends under the direction of Captain S.D. Campbell, who was a retired British Army officer living in Nelscott. The regular Army replaced the Beach Patrol after a year, but the AWS continued their observation duties until late in the war.

Militia at Newport. LCHS photo.

Kingfisher returns to civilian paint job. LCHS photo

In September of 1936, a major forest fire had burned through much of the Blodgett Tract. Some buildings in Camp 1 were burned, as were trestles and other structures on the railroad grades. The drainages of Big Creek, Vingie Creek, and Starr Creek burned. The Green Mountain area burned as far south as the Yachats River. The total area of the fire exceeded 10,000 acres. Most of the burned land was cut-over, so relatively little green timber was lost, although 500 acres of adjacent lands on the Siuslaw burned.[16]

As a result of the fire and poor logging practices, much of the Blodgett Tract was covered with partially burned snags and stumps, or ferns and brush. The natural seeding from mature trees left after logging could not take place since they were killed by the fire. Forest Supervisor Rex Wakefield entered into negotiations with the Spruce Corporation. In July 11, 1941, the Siuslaw completed purchase of the Tract for $99,947.14, and it became the Yachats Purchase Unit.[17]

The Unit desperately needed planting, road construction, and clean-up after the fire. In response, the Civilian Conservation Corps (CCC) built a camp there in 1941, called Camp Angell. In December, CCC Company 5436 moved into the new camp. The CCC began work on restoring the Unit in the spring of 1942, but by this time the U.S. had entered the war, and the CCC program was winding down. Company 5436 planted trees on 979 acres that spring.[18] During the summer, Camp Angell closed and the CCC planting crew disbanded.

In October, 1942, Civilian Public Service (CPS) men arrived, numbering 77 men by 1943. The CPS men were conscientious objectors who came from peace churches and political or philosophical groups, with some unaffiliated men. Forty-nine of the original men were members of the Church of the Brethren.

Rex Wakefield was the Forest Service administrator detailed to supervise the conservation work that the CPS men did. His memory of the CPS crew was mixed when he was interviewed in 1980 and 1989. Wakefield conceded that most of the men were willing workers, especially those with religious affiliations. Some political and philosophical "conchies" were less reliable, and some were actively hostile to physical labor. Wakefield reportedly advised these men to "go over the hill" and return to their homes.[19]

Camp Waldport was designated a Fine Arts camp. In addition to their conservation work, some of the men participated in activities including poetry, drama, music, printing, and other arts. The camp operated its own printing presses. Writers at Waldport included William Eversen (Brother Antoninius), Glen Coffield, Kenneth Patchen, William Sloan, and George Woodcock. Some of these men, most notably Everson and Patchen and the theater group went to San Francisco after the war and were active in the San Francisco Renaissance of the early 1950s. The Forest Service was apparently not

CPS men planting trees in Yachats Purchase Unit.

impressed with the poetry and drama, however, since they asked that fine arts men no longer be sent to Waldport.[20]

Through 1944 the CPS crew planted trees and did road work on the Yachats Purchase Unit. They eventually planted 9,000 acres with fir, spruce, and cedar from Forest Service nurseries. The country was rugged, roads were muddy, and the weather was coastal. Camp Waldport crews suffered five fatalities from accidents.[21] This was a significantly higher mortality rate than other CPS camps, and far greater than CCC camps.

Despite the heavy logging and fire that the Yachats Purchase Unit had suffered, some timber remained. The Siuslaw made two sales on the Unit during the war, one for $91,107 and the other for $88,315.[22] This was a tidy profit on the initial investment of $99,947.[23]

The war came to a close, and life returned to normal. Veterans came back to their jobs with the Forest Service and the lumber industry. The lookouts resumed their summer schedule, blackout curtains came down, and the conscientious objectors went home. With 10,000 acres of new trees, the old Blodgett Tract was healthier than before the war. Japanese mines continued to drift ashore for several years. Demolition teams blew them up harmlessly on the beach.

Close on the heels of World War II came the third major conflict of the twentieth century, usually called the "Cold War" between the western nations and the communist countries. The Siuslaw was less involved with the Cold War and the outbreaks in Korea and Vietnam than with the previous wars.

Despite the active hostilities in Korea and Vietnam, the Cold War was largely a technological chess match between the major powers. Each new military technology from the atomic bomb through the sophisticated anti-missile shields of the 1990s was matched by a newer technology, prolonging the military stalemate that lasted nearly 50 years. One important part of the military technology was electronic detection systems to prevent enemy aircraft from launching a surprise attack.

Mt. Hebo Airforce Radar Station, ca. 1956.

In 1953 the Army engineers planned and built a radar station on Mt. Hebo. The station was complete and operating by 1956.[24] This radar station was intended to provide early warning of approaching aircraft, which were considered a major threat to the U.S. at the time. After the Soviets detonated their first atomic bomb in 1950, the possibility of manned Soviet aircraft bombing the U.S. was taken seriously. Many communities established civil defense programs and air raid shelters. Ominously, the government re-established the WWII-vintage Ground Observer Corps.[25] Several radar systems were built in the 1950s, generally oriented to critical military installations like Hanford, Washington, or major population centers. Eventually, the completion of the Distant Early Warning (DEW) line across the Arctic made other radar installations redundant.[26] After 1957, with the Soviet development of intercontinental ballistic missiles, and their successful launch of the first satellite, the defense focus shifted from aircraft to missiles.

To judge from available documents, the Forest Service personnel on the Siuslaw had little interaction with the radar technicians at Mt. Hebo. The Forest's "Historical Notes for Calendar Year 1954" indicates that the military completed their barracks and the mess hall on the mountain and that they widened and paved the access road to the radar site in that year. Of course, the radar station was probably at least somewhat secret.

Additional facilities southeast of radar domes.

As the 1950s and 1960s passed, the Cold War became less of a concern until it finally ended with the dissolution of the Soviet Union in 1991. On a more personal level, Forester Clarence W. Jacobs recorded in his "Memories" that while he was working at the SO in the early 1950s he was trained and issued a "large packet of papers and brochures" about surviving a nuclear attack. The materials included information about building a fallout shelter, using a radiation detector, and coping with the "possible hostility and threat of friends and neighbors" who presumably did not have a fallout shelter or a radiation detector.[27]

NOTES

1 *The Timberman*, January 1917, 36.

2 Vernon Jensen, *Lumber and Labor* (New York, NY: Farrar and Rinehart, 1945) 125.

3 H.M. Hyman, *Soldiers and Spruce* (Los Angeles, CA: Institute of Industrial Relations, 1963) 110.

4 Lloyd Palmer, *Steam towards the Sunset* (Newport, OR: Lincoln County Historical Society, 1982) 33.

5 Disque Papers, General Orders, May 4-11, 1918.

6 Blodgett Papers, Brumby to Blodgett, April 14, 1915.

7 *United States Spruce Production Corporation Properties* (Portland, OR: 1919) 56.

8 B.A. Johnson and Archibald Whisnatt, *The Pacific Spruce Corporation* (Chicago, IL: Lumber World, 1924) 13.

9 Floyd R. Marsh, *Twenty Years a Soldier of Fortune* (Portland, OR: Binfords and Mort, 1976) 29.

10 Marsh, 29.

11 Marsh, 35.

12 Lawrence and Mary Rakestraw, *History of the Willamette National Forest* (on file, Eugene, OR: Willamette NF, 1975) 84.

13 Bill McCash, "The Aircraft Warning Service in World War II," *Waterways*, (Coos Bay, OR: Coos County Historical Society, September 2007) 3-6.

14 Bill McCash, "Forestry AWS Stations Activated During AWS Program" (on file, Waldport, OR: Siuslaw NF, n.d.). This material contains marked maps and lists of lookouts for the central Oregon coast with dates of AWS activation.

15 *Lincoln County Leader*, November 12, 1942.

16 Stephanie Finucane, *A History of the Blodgett Tract* (on file, Waldport, OR: Siuslaw NF, 1989) 34.

17 Finucane, 31.

18 Finucane, 32.

19 Finucane, 32; Wakefield Interview, 136-138.

20 Stephen D. Beckham, "Building 1381, Angell Job Corps Center" (on file, Corvallis, OR: Siuslaw NF, 1986) 8.

21 Beckham, 9.

22 Finucane, 36.

23 *Newport News Tribune*, November 16, 1947.

24 Rolfe Anderson, "Hebo District Historical Notes, 1907-1966" (on file, Waldport, OR: Siuslaw NF, n.d.).

25 David F. Winkler, "Searching the Skies" (www.fas.org/nuke/guide/usa/airdef/searching_the_skies.htm) 4.

26 Winkler, 7.

27 Clarence W. Jacobs, *Working in the Forest Supervisor's Office, Siuslaw National Forest"* (on file, Waldport, OR: Siuslaw NF, 1998).

CHAPTER FIVE

THE GREAT DEPRESSION

The Depression of the 1930s was a defining decade for the U.S. In parts of the Pacific Northwest, the Depression actually started a few years earlier than October, 1929, when the New York stock market collapsed. In Oregon, the lumber industry peaked during the 1920s, then went into a decline. Siuslaw National Forest timber sales reached 19.6 million board feet in 1924, then plunged to 1.9 million board feet in 1925. In 1926 sales climbed back to 12.3 million board feet, then fell below one million board feet in 1928 and remained at that level through the early 1930s.

Men from Resettlement Administration camp at Hebo Lake picnic shelter, ca. 1936.

The lumber industry was not the only business affected by the Depression. Manufacturing, retail, agriculture, and other businesses declined. On the Oregon coast, timber, fishing, and tourism drove the economy, and they were especially hard-hit. Historians have estimated that a third of American workers were out of work during these years. Unemployment numbers do not tell the whole story, for many Americans in the first decades of the twentieth century were self-employed farmers, tradesmen, or retail merchants. These people did not have jobs to lose, but they lost their businesses and their homes.

At the same time as the Depression—and intensifying its effect—an unrelated environmental disaster befell the Midwest and the Great Plains. This was the Dust Bowl, when drought and wind erosion destroyed farms throughout the region. The Pacific Northwest was affected by the Dust Bowl weather, and serious forest fires occurred on the coast in 1933 and 1936. Thousands of refugees forced off their lands in the Midwest made their way to California, Oregon, and Washington. As Depression-era novelist John Steinbeck wrote in *The Grapes of Wrath*, "the dispossessed were drawn west—from Kansas, Oklahoma, Texas" to the Pacific States.

The nation responded to the Depression through the social programs of the New Deal. After President Franklin D. Roosevelt's election in 1932, Congress passed a wide range of laws designed to put the unemployed to work, strengthen the nation's infrastructure of roads and bridges, reverse years of bad policies toward Native Americans, restore the Dust Bowl, teach conservation of natural resources, and curb the worst excesses of free-market capitalism. This was a tall order. Some of the New Deal programs were successes, some were failures, and most fell somewhere in between.

As an agency of the Department of Agriculture, the Siuslaw National Forest was involved in some of the largest programs of the New Deal. The Civilian Conservation Corps built roads, campgrounds, administrative buildings, and other infrastructure on the Forest. The Resettlement Administration purchased marginal farms in and around the Siuslaw, and those lands became part of the Forest. The Works Progress Administration (WPA) contributed to highway projects throughout western Oregon.

One enduring success of the New Deal on the Siuslaw and the Oregon coast was the completion of the U.S. 101, the Pacific Coast Highway. Funds from New Deal agencies, including the Reconstruction Finance Corporation (RFC), the Relief and Construction Act (RCA), and the Public Works Administration (PWA) paid for the highway and the major bridges. The new road linked the parts of the Siuslaw together, and opened the coast for logging and recreation as the economy improved.

Camp Nestucca was one of the permanent CCC camps on the Siuslaw.

Like other national forests, the Siuslaw also felt the influence of the New Deal in the National Industrial Recovery Act (NIRA) and its successor, the National Recovery Administration (NRA). The NRA regulated log prices, lumber prices, and lumber workers' wages through legislation known as the Lumber Code. Although the government's experiments in the lumber market were not entirely successful, a lasting benefit of the Lumber Code was Article X, which called for conservation and sustained yield management of national forests.

The Civilian Conservation Corps or CCC was one of the most ambitious programs of the New Deal. It was also one of the first New Deal programs, beginning in April of 1933. The program is closely identified with President Franklin Roosevelt because it was an idea that he had presented in his campaign. In essence, the CCC would enroll young men whose families were receiving public assistance. The young men would work on conservation projects on public lands for a basic wage of $30 per month. The Department of Labor was to provide personnel services for the CCC, including recruiting and finance. The Department of Defense would provide transportation, basic training, uniforms, and health care. The Forest Service, the National Park Service, and various state agencies would put the young men to work and supervise their activities.

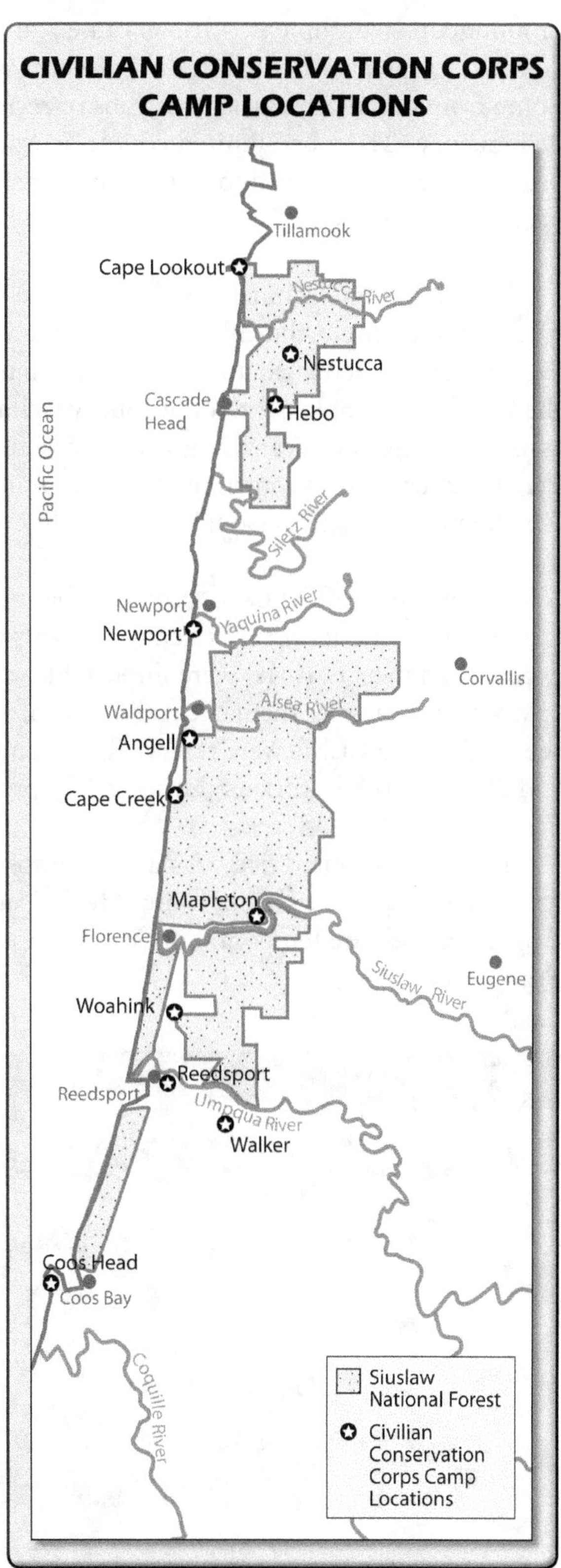

Over three million men enlisted in the CCC during its nine-year life. The CCC mobilized a larger number of young Americans than any government program before the World War II draft. The CCC was military in character. Army officers organized the recruits and put them into a para-military setting where they wore uniforms, lived in barracks, and worked under military discipline.

Young men came from many backgrounds and circumstances, from both rural and urban areas. Many had never seen a national forest, much less had any outdoor experience in a forest or mountain environment. Others came from the rural south, sons of tenant farmers and sharecroppers, who had lived in poverty, without adequate nutrition, for many years. Some from urban centers, lacking jobs or recreational opportunities, had drifted towards delinquency. Many had limited education, some to the point of illiteracy. As the CCC program matured, education in basic literacy and numeracy as well as vocational skills became a major focus.

In addition to teaching specific skills, the CCC program also taught certain social values. For example, the enlistees' allowance was officially set at $30 per month, but $25 of that was deducted and sent to their families, who were on relief. The wages of the CCC men supplemented the county welfare programs that offered their families assistance. The enlistees were given food, shelter, and occupation by the government, but they were required to contribute to their families' well-being, thus preserving a sense of family obligation and personal responsibility.

One element of the CCC program that was critical to its success was including local veterans and local craftsmen as mentors and leaders for the enlistees. These "local experienced men" (LEMs) were important for enculturating the enlistees into the world of work and teaching them the rudiments of various trades and crafts. In some instances, the skills of the LEMs were remarkable. Some of these men were masters of their trades, and like most other workers during the Depression, they were often unemployed.

The CCC operated five permanent camps on the Siuslaw National Forest. These were the Camp Cape Creek, Camp Hebo, Camp Mapleton, Camp Nestucca, and Camp Angell. There were temporary or "side" camps at numerous locations, including Marys Peak.

CCC men at Camp Cape Creek, Cape Perpetua.

THE IDEA BEHIND THE CCC

CCC men in camp after work, Camp Cape Creek.

President Roosevelt brought legislation to Congress in March of 1933 proposing the Civilian Conservation Corps. The CCC was to have dual purposes of financial relief for unemployed young men and conservation programs for public lands.[1] Roosevelt had an interest in conservation and forestry. His cousin, President Theodore Roosevelt was one of the first conservationists and is remembered as a powerful proponent of the forest reserves and the Forest Service.

This idea of conservation work for the unemployed was very much "in the air" during the early years of the Depression. In Europe, conservation projects operated in several countries. In 1932 as Governor of New York, Franklin D. Roosevelt had enlisted 10,000 unemployed men to plant trees in New York State Forests. When the Depression arrived in the Pacific Northwest, the Forest Service began operating conservation work camps for unemployed men.[2]

In Oregon and Washington, Region 6 cooperated with counties in establishing Subsistence Construction camps for unemployed men before the CCC was formed. Men could work for shelter, food, clothes, and tobacco. The Forest Service provided camping equipment, the counties provided funds, and the Forest Service assigned supervisors to coordinate work programs. The Siuslaw operated a Subsistence Construction camp in Lane County for 50 unemployed men.[3]

The CCC was to enlist "unmarried, idle men aged 18 to 25" for two purposes—to conduct conservation work and to provide employment. The relation of these two goals changed over time. At first, relief was primary:

Goals of the Civilian Conservation Corps

Goal 1	*Relief of unemployment, especially among young men*
Goal 2	*Health and attitude of enrollees*
Goal 3	*Relief of destitute families*
Goal 4	*Conservation projects*

CCC Manual, 1934

Ten years later, in 1944, relief had dropped to second place:

> *"The CCC program was looked on by many as a relief program rather than a conservation program. A good conservation program can do much toward the relief of the unemployed, but its main objective should never be thought of as relief."*
>
> *Conrad L. Wirth, "Final Report to the Secretary," 1944.*

Other goals were important too, especially goal #2 from the *CCC Manual*, which was the "Health and attitude of enrollees." In addition to the formal education programs that the CCC provided, it also offered opportunities for what many former enrollees refer to as "character building." The program took young men out of their homes and mixed them with men from different regions, ethnicities, religions, and cultures.

There are two tractor trailbuilders here, one "thirty cat" and a new "50" which arrived but ten days ago. These are being double shifted in order to get the maximum work done before the rain sets in.

***Six Twenty-Six*, September, 1933**

WHAT THE CCC ACCOMPLISHED

As interpreted by the CCC, conservation work often meant building roads and trails, constructing administrative buildings, and developing campgrounds. On the Siuslaw, as on other national forests, CCC crews also contributed to reforestation and fire fighting, although these activities had a 20-year history on the Forest before the CCC. Other CCC conservation work included insect control programs, erosion control, flood control, range improvements, and some work with wildlife habitat restoration.

The work projects of this company are confined primarily to the Siuslaw National Forest. They are under the direction of the Supervisor of the Forest and the Ranger of the Hebo Ranger District. Types of projects vary with the seasons. During the summer practically all work ceases and the time is taken up fighting forest fires. Winter is the planting season. Road construction and improvement goes on throughout the year as do the various building projects. In the spring the telephone lines to the lookout stations must be repaired and put in shape for fire season and foot trails cleared and repaired.

Coast Range Beacon **CCC Camp Nestucca, Blaine, Oregon, Company 5436, 1940**

Captain K.E. Kevenen at Camp Mapleton.

Planting and Pruning The planting of 200,000 Douglas fir seedlings was completed November 19. The work was started October 29 by a crew from the Nestucca CCC camp. This planting is a continuation of the planting begun on the Kay Burn in 1910. The total plantation now covers an area of 10,000 acres.

Six Twenty-Six**, December, 1935**

Accomplishments of Company 5436 at Camp Nestucca

Since its arrival at Camp Nestucca, Company 5436 has put in an average of more than 3500 man days per month of projects. Listed below are a few of the accomplishments:

- 2,100 man days constructing 3 bridges.
- 6,500 man days constructing 6 buildings of all types and sizes
- Construction of 21 miles of telephone lines and maintenance of 43 miles
- Construction of 5 ½ miles of truck trails and maintenance of 50 miles. Not included in this is the gravelling of a road from Blaine towards camp, a distance of about five miles to date. Gravel for this was crushed and the crusher operated by the enrollees of the Company.
- Maintenance of 30 miles of foot trail and construction of a mile of new trail.
- Improvement of 346 acres of forest stand. This includes pruning selected trees in order that they will produce a better grade of lumber when they mature.
- 900 acres of land has been planted in forest trees.
- 2,200 man days have been spent on fire prevention and pre-suppression.
- 6,060 man days have been spent in fighting forest fires, not only in the immediate vicinity of this camp but also in other areas of Oregon and Washington.
- 900 man days have been spent improving and constructing public campgrounds.
- 29 man days have been spent on survey.

Coast Range Beacon, CCC Camp Nestucca, Company 5436, 1940

CCC BUILDING AND DESIGN

The distinctive CCC structures on the Siuslaw and other national forests of the Pacific Northwest are perhaps the most visible legacy of the program. CCC structures included buildings for forest management and public recreation.

Standards and plans for Forest Service buildings in the CCC construction program were provided in the *Improvement Handbook*, published in 1937 and later supplemented by *Acceptable Plans for Forest Service Administrative Buildings*, published in 1939. These two books offered sample plans, specifications of material, and suggestions for choosing appropriate sites. The books promoted a style that was sometimes called "Government Rustic." It was popular during the 1920s and 1930s for park buildings, cabins, and lodges.

The CCC built the Ranger's residence at the Waldport Ranger Station.

As Forest Service historian Gail Throop points out, the Rustic Style had no single point of origin in architectural history. Influences include the British and American romantics, like Andrew Jackson Downing, and such original American designers as Gustav Stickley, Frederick Law Olmstead, and Bernard Maybeck.[4]

The Rustic Style also derives from vernacular building traditions in wood and stone. In 1934, President Roosevelt's friend and Secretary of the Interior, Harold Ickes, realized that the CCC and other New Deal programs would be making an unprecedented contribution to the infrastructure of parks and other public lands in the U.S. Ickes assigned National Park Service architect Albert H. Good and his staff to prepare a book explaining the Rustic Style and offering examples of successful buildings and outdoor facilities designed in this style. The Department of the Interior published the first edition of *Park Structures and Facilities* in 1935. A second edition was available after 1938.

Good defined the Rustic Style as "a style which, through the use of native materials in proper scale, and through the avoidance of straight lines and over sophistication, gives the feeling of having been executed by pioneer craftsmen with limited hand tools. It thus achieves sympathy with natural surroundings and with the past."[5]

Waldport Ranger Station complex was a CCC building project.

The goal of sympathy with natural setting and with the Euro-American past was, of course, exactly the kind of value statement that was appropriate to the Civilian Conservation Corps program. In the Pacific Northwest, this style took the form of wooden frame buildings with fieldstone masonry. The siding of the buildings often combined two or more textures, including horizontal clapboard, vertical board and batten, shingles, shakes, and various patterns of drop siding. Roof pitches tended to be steep. Roofing material was usually cedar shingle. The fieldstone masonry generally included the exposed foundation of the building, and also the entry, patio, and chimneys. Outdoor fireplaces were common, as were other stone hardscape features. Ornamental elements included timber brackets at doorways and entries, and wooden shutters with the familiar Forest Service conifer cutout.

Staff residence in the bungalow style, Waldport.

Windows were a signature design element on CCC Forest Service buildings in Region 6. These were generously used on most buildings. They were always mullioned windows with multiple lights that gave the buildings a distinctly "cottage-like" look. Window surrounds were typically wide and often ornamented with moulding. Paint or stain schemes favored earth-tones, especially brown stain in forested areas. Buildings in the open could be grey or white. The Ranger's houses at Waldport and Mapleton are excellent examples of CCC residential design.

Rock work needs first of all to be in proper scale. The average size of rocks employed must be sufficiently large to justify the use of masonry. Rocks should be placed on their natural beds, the stratification of the bedding planes horizontal, never vertical. Variety of size lends interest and results in a pattern far more pleasing than that produced by units of common or nearly common size. Informality vanishes from rock work if the rocks are laid in courses like brick work or of the horizontal joints are not broken. In walls, the larger rocks should be used near the base and by no means should smaller ones be used exclusively in the upper portions. Rather should a variety of sizes be common to the whole surface, the larger predominating at the base. Rocks should be selected for color and hardness.

Albert H. Good, *Park Structures and Facilities*, 1935

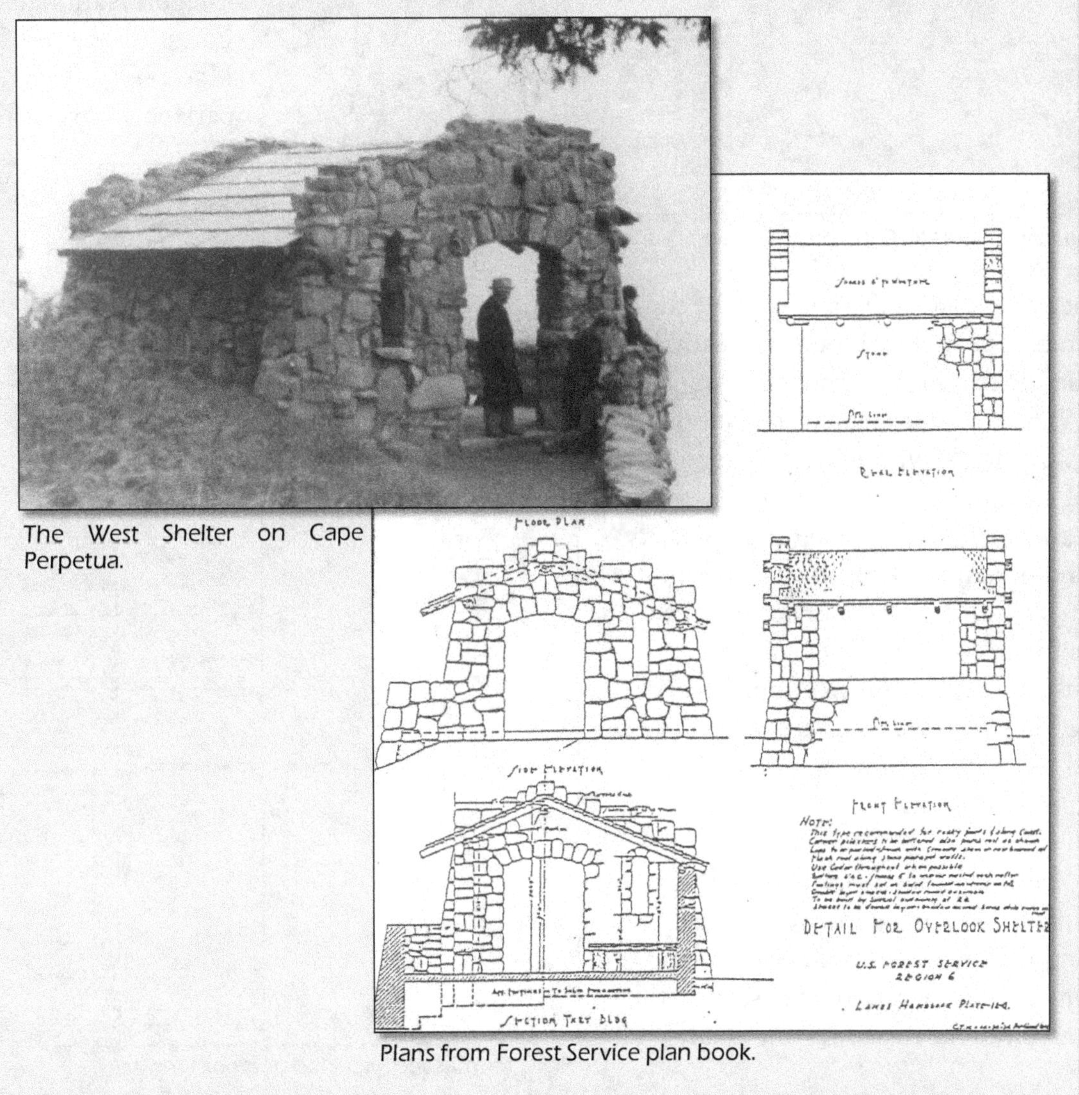

The West Shelter on Cape Perpetua.

Plans from Forest Service plan book.

Campground structures were especially important in the CCC building program. In the 1930s, outdoor recreation for the American public was rapidly gaining popularity and significance. The Forest Service began its recreation program in earnest after March 4, 1915, when Congress passed the Term Occupancy Act. This allowed national forests to make public lands available to private parties who wanted to build lodges, resorts, or cabins.

Building fireplace, Cape Perpetua campground.

In the same year, the Forest Service created the Columbia River Gorge Park on the Oregon National Forest (now the Mt. Hood NF). This park encompassed nearly 14,000 acres, and was the most ambitious national forest recreation facility to date.[6] In the following year, 1916, Congress created the National Park Service within the Department of the Interior to manage the national parks that were growing in popularity and becoming oases for recreation. In 1917, the Forest Service engaged landscape architect Fred Waugh to investigate forest recreation. His report, *Recreational Uses of the National Forests*, was the first agency-wide approach to this topic.

During the 1920s, national forest recreation grew in popularity and the Forest Service struggled to provide campgrounds, trails, and other amenities for the recreating public.

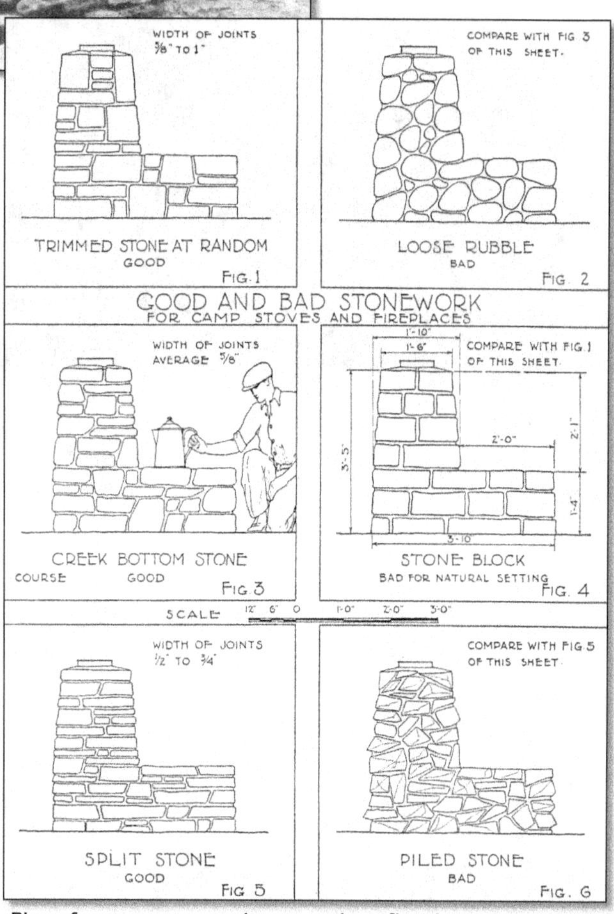

Plans for masonry work on outdoor fireplaces.

When the Depression came along, recreation slowed slightly, and the agency was able to catch its breath. As CCC labor and resources became available after 1933, recreation development was a priority for the Forest Service.

The CCC put its distinctive stamp on the recreation facilities it built. Here, as with other CCC building projects, the aesthetic of the Rustic Style prevailed. National Park Service architect Albert Good devoted 10 of the 21 chapters in his book *Park Structures and Facilities* to outdoor amenities including signs, walls, steps, seats and tables, fireplaces and camp stoves, and entrance ways. His designs emphasized native stone and timber construction, with a careful eye to craftsmanship and proper scale and proportions.

Finishing outdoor fireplace.

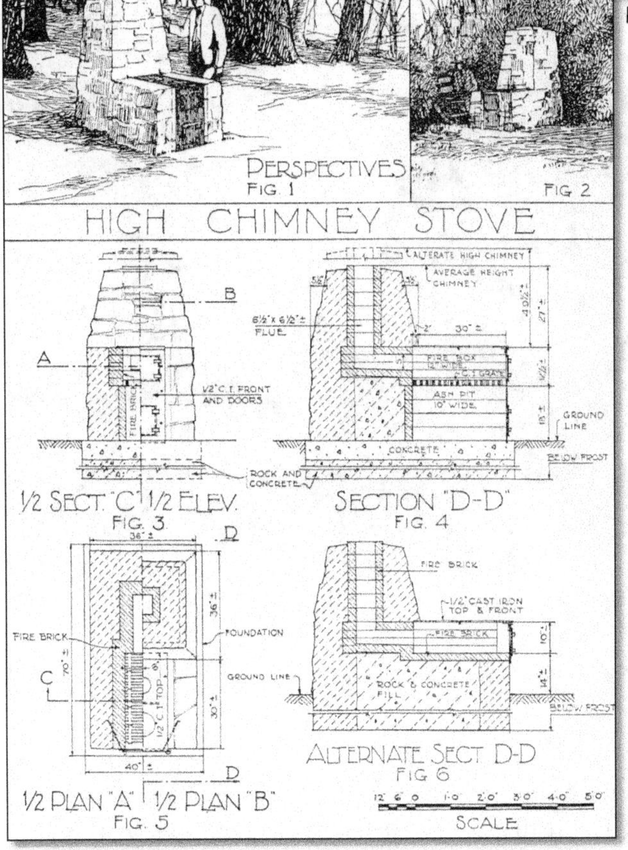

Outdoor fireplace plans, Forest Service plan book, 1937.

The CCC built several campgrounds on the Siuslaw, but the crown jewel was the complex at Cape Perpetua. The stonework on the walls and parapet, the trails and trail shelter are excellent examples of the CCC design and craft. The West Shelter, built in 1933, shows influences of the trail shelters featured in *Park Structures and Facilities.* Plans for this shelter were published in the Forest Service Region 6 *Lands Handbook.*

In its nine-year life on the Siuslaw, the Civilian Conservation Corp built and occupied five permanent camps—Camp Cape Creek, Camp Hebo, Camp Mapleton, Camp Nestucca, and Camp Angell. Temporary "side camps" or "spike camps" were built at several locations and used only for the duration of a specific construction project.

Photos of the camps show plain, utilitarian buildings arranged in rows and squares. While the CCC crews lavished their best building skills on the buildings intended for public or administrative uses, their camp buildings were temporary and intentionally plain.

Structures used for the CCC camps included three broad categories: tents, frame buildings, and portable buildings. In general the first camps were tent camps, and these were replaced with "all-weather" camps, usually of frame buildings. After 1937 all CCC camps were to be built with portable buildings. These were buildings assembled from wall units built in factories. The portable buildings could be assembled by unskilled crews on site, and then could be disassembled and moved when the camps were abandoned. The military had developed these portable buildings as "portable cantonments."

CCC Camp Nestucca on Clarence Creek.

The CCC frame buildings were built without a perimeter foundation. They were typically set on wooden sills or on posts. The walls were platform framed and sheathed with nominal one inch shiplap sheathing. Roofing was composition roll roofing, and

CCC Camp Cape Creek at Cape Perpetua.

windows and doors were conventional units. The standard buildings for a permanent camp included eight different kinds of separate structures:

Mess hall
Recreation hall
Infirmary
Officers' quarters
Truck garage
Latrine
Shower house[7]

Photos of Camp Nestucca show rows of frame buildings with cupolas. The buildings are sided with tar paper secured with vertical battens. Two of the buildings—the office or headquarters—are shingled. The Camp Cape Creek features barracks elevated at the downhill end and joined at the rear (uphill) with covered walkways.

THE END OF THE CCC

As the 1930s ended, the U.S. moved closer to prosperity and to joining the war in Europe. Military enlistment and lower welfare rolls meant that fewer young men were eligible for the CCC. The organization had problems finding enough recruits. Finally in December, 1941, the U.S. entered the war, and in June of 1942, the CCC program officially ended.

CCC camps were dismantled, and the building parts moved to military installations. Some camps were re-used by the military. The camp at Big Creek became the Waldport CPS camp and this site is still in use as the Angell Job Corps camp. Many of the CCC enrollees entered the military, where their training prepared them for various specialties.

> **Within the last six months the Siuslaw group has held seven gatherings for its members: Three farewell gatherings, three newly-wed gatherings, and one dance for general principles.**
>
> ***Six Twenty-Six*, August, 1935**

THE RESETTLEMENT ADMINISTRATION

One of President Roosevelt's priorities for the New Deal in 1933 was to help the victims of the Dust Bowl. These people had lost their farms in the Midwest and South during the late 1920s and were relocating to other parts of the country as seasonal farm workers. Most of the Dust Bowl farms were dry farms in land too arid to grow cereal crops during the drought years of the late 1920s.

New Deal programs for the rural poor began with the Division of Subsistence Homesteads (1933-1934), then changed to the Rural Rehabilitation Division (1934-1935), then the Resettlement Administration (1935-1937), and finally the Farmers' Home Administration (1937-1994). In the Midwest, these organizations acquired lands abandoned by farmers, and put the lands into several conservation and reclamation programs, including the national grasslands. The Bankhead-Jones Farm Tenant Act (July 22, 1937) was the enabling legislation for creating national grasslands, federal wildlife refuges, and adding lands to the national forests, including the Siuslaw. Specifically, the Act directed the Secretary of Agriculture to develop a program of land conservation "to correct maladjustments in land use and assist in such things as reforestation and the protection of fish and wildlife and natural resources."[8]

President Roosevelt created the Resettlement Administration (RA) by Executive Order 7027 on May 1, 1935. The new agency had three main tasks:

A) to resettle destitute or low-income families from rural or urban areas,
B) to initiate conservation projects for soil erosion, stream pollution, seacoast erosion, reforestation, and flood control, and
C) to lend money to help farmers or farm tenants purchase lands or equipment.

A forth provision of the Act empowered the new agency to acquire by purchase or eminent domain farms, ranches, or timber lands. The agency could then sell this real estate or transfer it to other government agencies.

RA appraiser and surveyor at the Cape Creek CCC camp during the Resettlement Administration years, 1936.

Although Oregon's Coast Range was certainly not part of the Dust Bowl, there was widespread rural poverty and subsistence farming. The Resettlement Administration created the Western Oregon Scattered Settlers Project, and opened offices in Eugene and Tillamook. The project solicited participation by subsistence farmers who were willing to sell their lands at the prices the program was paying.

APR 3 1935

Form SW-33
(Revised)

To the owners of submarginal land within the boundaries of Western Oregon Scattered Settler Project, Oregon A-2:

You probably know something about the submarginal land program; I am glad to advise that this program is available to you if you and your neighbors are sufficiently interested; if not, it is planned to transfer it elsewhere.

I want to tell you something about this opportunity.

You may option your land to the Government at an appraised price, this price to be paid directly to you in due time in order that you may make a home elsewhere without assistance; or the option price in some cases may be applied as first payment on good resettlement land, located nearer to schools, purchased by the Government for you and improved and stocked in a way to assist you in making a living and paying for the tract over a term of years. Liberal terms are being offered. See project manager of resettlement area if you want Government aid in relocating.

We all know that land prices are down, and in appraising the lands you own values will also be low. Non-tillable lands covered with fern, down logs and brush are seldom appraised higher than $1.00 an acre. Timbered lands may be appraised as high as $7.50 an acre. Cultivated land and improvements such as buildings, fences, etc., will be given a fair appraisal, taking into consideration age, character and a proper depreciation charge. No average figure can be given. If you would like to have more information let me know what questions you would like to have answered.

If you want an examination and appraisal made, fill out the enclosed form SL-05 Revised and send it to Project Manager at

~~101 Court House,~~ Tillamook, Oregon,
or
430 Miner Building, Eugene, Oregon.

A number of people have taken advantage of this opportunity, and those who are interested should act promptly, since funds available are limited by act of congress, and it will not be possible to extend this offer to all. If you are not interested in any way in this proposal, please let me know so that the money can be used elsewhere.

Please understand that my desire and the desire of the Federal Government is to help you and if you require no assistance and are fully satisfied and intend to remain where you are, just let me know and no appraisal will be made.

Yours very truly,

R S Shelley

R. S. SHELLEY,
Project Manager, Oregon A-2

In Reply Refer to

Enclosure

Forest Supervisor Ralph Shelley was re-assigned to lead the Resettlement Administration Program in western Oregon.

As "scattered settlers" from Coast Range homesteads sold their lands into the program, they were moved off the land and into Resettlement Administration camps established in conjunction with CCC camps at Mapleton, Nestucca, and Cape Creek, plus eight side camps. Men in the camps continued CCC projects and built guard stations at Alsea, Big Elk, and Vincent Creek.

Through the agency of the Bankhead-Jones Act, 69,482 acres of timberlands and sub-marginal farm land acquired by the Resettlement Administration became part of the Siuslaw National Forest in 1940.[9] At the same time, lands acquired by the government through two other New Deal programs—the National Industrial Recovery Act and the Emergency Relief Appropriation Act—were added to the Forest.

Much of the controversy surrounding the Resettlement Administration comes from the perception that the government was perhaps too aggressive in removing impoverished settlers from their lands. Documents like the solicitation letter show that the agency was careful not to coerce settlers, and that it offered the going price for land, albeit at Depression prices. There is no doubt that the program worked better on the Midwest farms than it did in the Oregon Coast Range. A study prepared by the Department of Agriculture in 1941, after the end of the program, took a negative view towards resettlement in the Oregon Coast Range:

> An extreme instance of isolated agricultural population is to be found in the coastal mountains of western Oregon. Here, scattered small farm units cluster in those few places where the narrow, twisted stream valleys widen sufficiently so that a few acres of arable bottom lands are to be found. These isolated farms and small neighborhoods of farms are located along the lengths and usually far back toward the headwaters of virtually all the numerous streams draining this rugged, mountainous coastal area.
>
> After a resettlement program was inaugurated and it was well along toward completion, in an adjacent area, the Oregon Land Grant College Bureau of Agricultural Economics Committee, contemplating possible extension of such programs, began to feel the need for new criteria for determining the desirability of land retirement and resettlement as applied to the populations of isolated mountain areas. Some of the removed families reappeared in the mountains. Others were reported not successful in adjusting to new environments.
>
> Thus certain questions arose: Were there social factors to be found among such people which should modify purely economic decisions as to the need for retirement of remote lands from agricultural uses? Had the residents of these lands, living under conditions of relative insulation from the processes of social change, developed or retained social values at variance with those prevalent in more accessible districts? And were such differences if they did exist of such character and magnitude as to influence the desirability of resettlement on more productive and less isolated farms? ...Were actual living conditions enough below their standards of living to make them seriously dissatisfied with what they had and willing to accept different environments and different farm practices in return for higher levels of living?[10]

The author answered his own questions a few pages later:

> [Among] these mountain populations, then, ...pioneer traditions are strong. ... In such cases there is considerable reason to believe, resettlement, if it involved

removal from accustomed valleys and breaking family ties, would produce more social maladjustment and problems than it would remedy.

The opposing point of view is apparent in a note prepared by men in the Resettlement Administration Camp Mapleton in 1936. They set their note adrift in a bottle. Their attitude is that they are participating in history, and that they are "marching hand in hand with the Democratic and progressive leadership of Franklin D. Roosevelt" to overcome adversities met by "man in every walk of life during the past few years."

Mapleton, Oregon
April 12th.1936

The men listed below are employees of the Resettlement Adminstration at Camp Mapleton,Mapleton,Oregon.And who are marching hand in hand with the Democratic and progressive leadership of Franklin.D.Roosevelt.To over come the adversities met by man in every walk of life during the past few years.And we sincerally hope that the finder of this bottle and the members of his generation will be bobbling about on the sea of life in all the luxeries that this world of ours can so eaisly afford.And for which we are so earnestly striving to set on its march of progress.Feeling sure that by the time that this bottle is found that the wheels of industries,will be humming as they have never hummed before.And it is with this confidence.That we are proud to be in aposition to be members of the camp laying this corner stone in honor of the men who have striven honestly to help lighten the burden of his fellow man.

Ira.E.Jones,Division Engineer
Chas.L.Blanding,Project Supt
~~[illegible]~~ foreman
Earl Gallup,foreman
Riley Thomson,foreman
Carl Dragoo,Foreman
Earnest Greenhagen,foreman
A.G.Hines"slim",foreman
A.R.Major, ~~[illegible]~~ Steward
Elmer Mathews,Chef
Herbert Dukes,Bookkeeper
Paul Petersen,Timekeeper
Allen Dorr,Store keeper
Charles Wallace,Sub foreman
Walter.L.Smith,Sub foreman
Lee Prentice,First Aid
J.G.Winningham,First Aid
Lawrence Denny Truck driver
Harry Thurston,Carpentier helper
Duane Fulmer,truck driver

District Ranger

This is written with both ink and type writter,so if age should deteriate one the other might last the devastages of age

Note sent in a bottle from Camp Mapleton, 1936.

MAJOR 1930S BRIDGES BY CONDE B. MCCULLOUGH FOR THE COAST HIGHWAY PROJECT

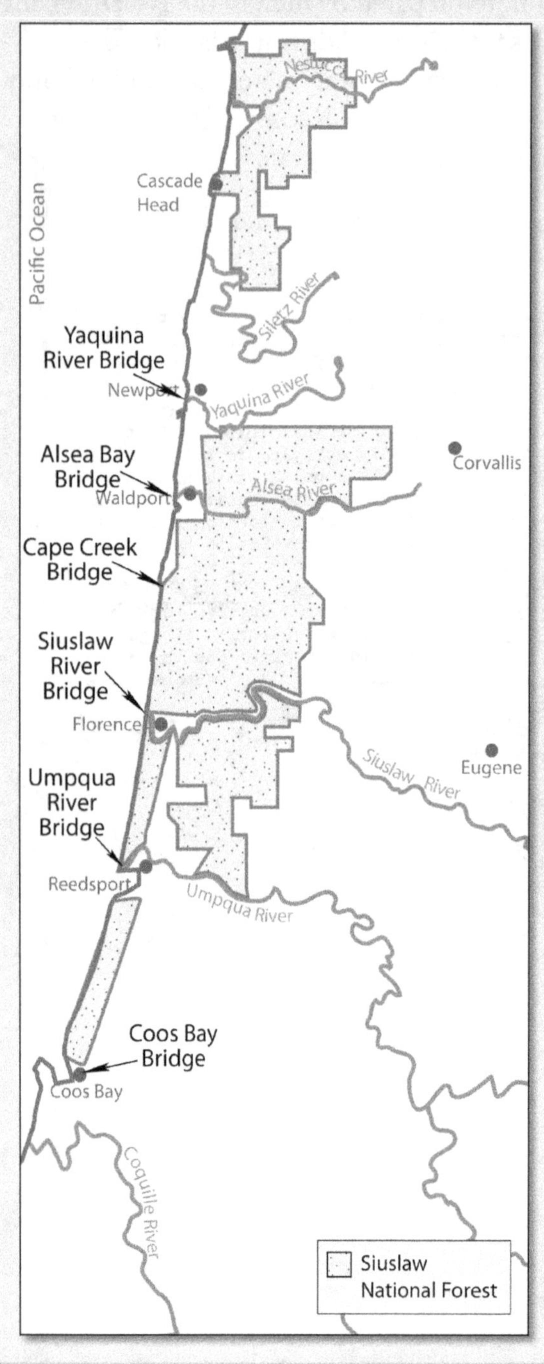

Completing the Coast Highway and turning it into a viable route for commerce and tourism was a New Deal project that had important impacts on the Siuslaw National Forest. Prior to the project, the north-south route along the coast was a slow, wandering country road. The quality of the road varied. River crossings required a ferry or a long detour inland. Improvement of the coast route was a priority for the Oregon State Highway Department through the 1920s. California was completing its "Redwood Highway," which was invigorating the coastal economy and bringing isolated coastal communities into the twentieth century. Oregon wanted to follow suit, so advocates of the new highway formed the Oregon Coast Highway Association to make their case in Salem in the 1920s.

With the end of the prosperous 1920s and the onset of the Depression, the future of the new highway for the Oregon coast looked bleak. The coast highway would be extremely expensive to build

Yaquina River bridge under construction.

because of the need for bridges, tunnels, and cantilevered roads on the rocky headlands. The first major bridge was built on the Siuslaw National Forest at Heceta Head across Cape Creek in 1932. The bridge required an accompanying 700 foot tunnel. The cost earned this portion of the highway the name "the million dollar mile."[11]

Blasting for highway around Cape Perpetua.

In 1933, the Oregon State Highway Department applied for federal funds through the newly-created Public Works Administration (PWA). PWA projects were to employ workers and improve the nation's infrastructure. The PWA provided grants to the Highway Department and loans which were repaid with gasoline tax revenues.

The Highway Department's strategy for the central coast called for major bridges at Coos Bay, Reedsport, Florence, Waldport, and Newport. These bay and river crossings were served by ferries, meaning long waits and unpredictable service in bad weather. Conde B. McCullough was the Oregon State Highway Department bridge engineer. By 1932 McCullough's bridges throughout Oregon's highway system had won considerable notice. The five coast bridges—plus the Cape Creek bridge at Heceta Head—

Cape Creek bridge, 1932 at Heceta Head.

would earn him a place as one of the nation's premier bridge designers. McCullough's use of concrete and steel arches is probably unrivaled among American bridge architects. The combination of catenary arches and Roman arches that characterizes the Yaquina River bridge and the Cape Creek bridge is striking and aesthetically effective.

NOTES

1 John A. Salmond, *The Civilian Conservation Corps, 1933-1942: A New Deal Case Study* (Durham, NC: Duke University, 1967) 4.

2 Lawrence and Mary Rakestraw, *A History of the Willamette National Forest* (Eugene, OR: Willamette NF, 1975) 75.

3 *Six Twenty-Six*, March, 1933.

4 E. Gail Throop, "Utterly Visionary and Chimerical; A Federal Response to the Depression. An Examination of Civilian Conservation Corps Construction on National Forest Lands in the Pacific Northwest." (MA Thesis, Portland, OR: Portland State University, 1979).

5 Albert H. Good, *Park Structures and Facilities* (Washington, DC: USGPO, 1935) 3-4.

6 Throop, 4.

7 Alison T. Otis, William Honey, Thomas C. Hogg, and Kimberly Lakin, *The Forest Service and the Civilian Conservation Corps, 1933-1942* (Corvallis, OR: USDA Forest Service, 1986) 73.

8 Act of July 22, 1937. 50 Stat 525.

9 Sidney Baldwin, *Poverty and Politics: The Rise and Decline of the Farm Security Administration* (Chapel Hill, NC: University of North Carolina, 1968) 163.

10 Michael R. Hanger, "The Farm People of Isolated Areas in Lincoln and Western Benton Counties, Oregon." (Berkeley, CA: USDA Bureau of Agricultural Economics, 1941) 1.

11 Robert W. Hadlow, *Elegant Arches, Soaring Spans* (Corvallis, OR: Oregon State University, 2001) 85.

CHAPTER SIX

TIMBER ON THE SIUSLAW

TIMBER

When Euro-Americans first entered the central Oregon coast country in the 1850s, they found a substantial volume of standing timber and an environment that offered an amazing potential for growing more timber. The combination of ample rain, mild temperatures, and deep forest soil favored the growth of Douglas fir, western red cedar, Sitka spruce, and western hemlock among the conifers, and red alder, big leaf maple, cascara, and other deciduous species. It was, as the saying goes, "natural timber country." On the other hand, the land was not well suited for farming. The hills were too steep to farm and the few arable creek-bottom lands were narrow and shaded.

Mixed-age stand of coast country conifers.

As a result, early settlers were often more interested in timber than agriculture. They claimed the best timber lands before the turn of the century by a variety of legal and not entirely legal means. By the time the forest reserves and the Siuslaw National Forest were formed in 1907 and 1908, the lands remaining in the public domain were less attractive than the lands already claimed. What remained to become the Siuslaw National Forest

> **A large part of the old-growth timber that escaped the fire [of the 1840s] did not escape the timber seekers who also own a vast amount of second-growth fir as well. Some of these areas [of old-growth fir] are still under public ownership.... However, no large bodies are the case, and they lie, for the most part, scattered throughout.**
>
> ***Siuslaw National Forest Land Classification Atlas*, 1919**

were burned-over lands, second growth timber, and the barren sand dunes south of Florence. Yet, these lands are usually counted within the top five percent of all timber-growing lands in the U.S. Most estimates place the original timber standing on the Siuslaw as 80 to 85 percent second growth, 20 to 70 years old.[1] The timber standing on the Siuslaw was initially estimated at four billion board feet on a land base of roughly 500,000 acres. In 1980, after years of heavy cutting, the standing timber was estimated at over seven billion board feet.

> **The destructive fires of early days very definitely placed the Siuslaw in the deferred income class. No large body of old-growth remained which could provide an extensive long-term logging operation with consequent large receipts. Oases of mature timber in varying size were left here and there, but only those accessible to water logging were touched prior to the comparatively recent advent of truck logging.**
>
> ***A History of the Siuslaw National Forest, Oregon, as of December 31, 1939***

Until World War II, the Siuslaw National Forest sold little timber, usually less than five million board feet per year. Sales in the 1920s and 1930s were mostly to individual users or small neighborhood mills. A significant lumber industry was growing in the coastal portions of Tillamook, Lincoln, Lane, and Coos counties at this time. These mills were well-supplied with their own proprietary timber, and it was often better quality than the timber available on the national forest. Also, the national forest timber was difficult to reach. The timber growing along rivers suitable for navigation or driving logs was in private ownership. Inland timber could be logged by rail, but that required significant investment.

Forty years later, several factors had combined to favor large national forest timber sales. First, the post-war housing boom increased the demand for lumber. Second, the private timber reserves were rapidly declining. Third, truck and tractor logging technology, coupled with better roads, was making more national forest timber accessible. Finally, trees that grew after the huge fires of the 1840s were now over 100 years old and reaching maturity.

The lumber industry on the coast cut logs on private lands in the 1860s and 1870s, but began logging national forest lands after World War II. Many of the lands that were logged in private ownership early in the century became part of the Siuslaw in later years.

HISTORICAL SOLD AND HARVESTED VOLUMES

For The Siuslaw National Forest From 1915-1979

Volumes are in millions of board feet (MMBF) and include convertible products.

Year	Volume in MMBF	
	Sold	Harvested
1915	0.1	0.2
1916	0.2	0.3
1920	12.3	5.5
1921	28.8	8.2
1922	11.4	11.5
1923	11.4	9.8
1924	29.6	16.0
1925	1.9	5.1
1926	12.3	5.2
1927	5.0	10.2
1928	0.8	7.6
1929	2.4	0.9
1930	0.2	1.0
1931	0.5	0.3
1932	0.7	0.4
1933	0.2	0.4
1934	0.4	0.3
1935	3.0	0.4
1936	3.7	1.0
1937	1.3	2.6
1938	4.7	2.2
1939	7.3	3.3
1940	2.4	6.5
1941	7.4	5.6
1942	32.1	8.9
1943	13.8	37.2
1944	38.6	26.3
1945	69.0	27.4
1946	27.2	62.0
1947	103.5	57.6
1948	34.4	85.9
1949	29.5	55.2

Year	Volume in MMBF	
	Sold	Harvested
1950	77.5	50.4
1951	50.9	58.6
1952	98.3	79.6
1953	113.6	122.9
1954	193.9	129.2
1955	230.9	182.4
1956	238.6	177.2
1957	213.8	206.0
1958	326.4	56.5
1959	304.9	334.0
1960	335.1	355.7
1961	344.5	307.5
1962	361.6	335.2
1963	593.7	388.9
1964	354.0	461.6
1965	366.5	412.1
1966	383.8	397.2
1967	373.1	301.2
1968	378.7	395.7
1969	379.3	377.2
1970	355.0	238.5
1971	360.2	333.5
1972	389.4	356.6
1973	368.9	420.4
1974	305.9	365.5
1975	296.3	231.5
1976	328.1	294.2
*FY 100	23.4	70.6
FY 77	299.5	332.2
FY 78	373.4	314.9
FY 79	349.6	374.4

*FY 100 is the 3 month period when the fiscal year changed to start October 1.

Annual cut 1915-1979, Siuslaw National Forest.

The earliest lumber mills in the coast country served local markets with lumber for houses, barns, and other homestead structures. On the upper Alsea, the Ruble mill, the Lone Star mill, and the Inman mill cut lumber through the 1870s and 1880s for settlers in the area, and for shipment to the Willamette Valley by wagon and team.[2] Hauling lumber to the Valley for sale required a fortunate combination of good prices and roads dry enough to be passable.

Log on bull chain, C.A. Smith mill, Coos Bay. C.P. Cronk photo, 1910-1911.

On Yaquina Bay, George Megginson built a mill at Depot Slough in 1867, and Benjamin Simpson built a mill near Yaquina City in 1871 which reportedly could cut 20 thousand board feet (MBF) each day. The first mill on Tillamook Bay was the Baxter mill, located near Idaville. On the lower Alsea, the Baldwin mill at Waldport was cutting lumber by the 1880s, and a competing mill at Tidewater was also producing lumber at this time.

Small mill cutting fir. C.P. Cronk photo, 1910-1911.

The technology of the early mills was relatively simple. The mills were steam powered. The head rig was typically a circular saw, usually with inserted teeth and occasionally mounted with a second circular saw to form a "top-and-bottom" head rig. This configuration could cut large logs by cutting from the top of the log and the bottom of the log in a single curf. Head-rig carriages were often pulled by horses. Edging was also done on the head-rig. There was typically no planer, and no dry kiln. Green lumber was stacked in the rain to season.

Logging technology during the early years relied on gravity and muscle power. After the loggers felled trees, they bucked them into logs that they could move with jacks to a

Gravity chute bringing logs down to a landing, ca. 1880s.

log chute or skid trail. The chutes were made of smooth poles placed across the route of the log. Some chutes were steep enough to move the logs downhill by gravity, and some required oxen or horses to provide additional power. In certain favored locations, nineteenth century loggers on the coast were able to use streams to drive the logs down to tidewater. These streams required splash dams to build up a head of water. When the dam was released, the rush of water washed the logs downstream.

My mother's father, Stephen Hoover, logged with oxen, moving much of the prime timber around Waldport and upriver. Henry Nice logged near the mouth of Drift Creek with Cal Barned driving the animals. Cal, a kindly, soft spoken man could coax more work from an oxen than with cussing and yelling. If one of the crew raised his voice, the animals lurched forward, usually breaking the chains and causing extra work.

In order to get the logs into the river, jack screws, skid roads, and chutes were devised. Canyons sometimes served as chutes by being lined with heavy peeled poles. Mud dragged down acted as grease. Sometimes in dry weather, the chutes would actually be greased with axle lubricant.

Marjorie H. Hays, *The Land That Kept Its Promise*

Splash dam on a stream near the Coos River estuary. C.P. Cronk photo, 1910-1911.

The river was the exclusive mode of log transportation until a network of roads came on the scene. The further up the river one tried to float logs, the more difficult the job became because of the river's small size and the numerous bends. To give the logs an extra boost, at least one splash dam was used in the early 1920s...The logs were yarded to form cold decks and these decks were then yarded into the river behind the dam. During a freshet of high water, a steam donkey would pull the dam apart, causing a surge of water to carry the logs down the river.

N. Judd Huntington and Wally Holden Interviews, 1994

Most of the early mills were limited to selling lumber in local markets or to nearby markets that could be reached by wagon and team. Another group of mills was designed to produce lumber that would be shipped by sea to distant markets. These mills were called cargo mills because of their reliance on cargo vessels to move their product to market. The best-known of these was the Gardiner Mill Company at Gardiner, near the confluence of the Umpqua and Smith rivers. Built in 1864 to supply lumber to California, the Gardiner mill came under the ownership of Coos Bay lumberman Asa M. Simpson in 1868. By the turn of the century, the Gardiner mill was cutting around 20 million board feet of lumber each year.[3]

Four-masted lumber schooner. C.P. Cronk photo, 1910-1911.

Other cargo mills were operating on Coos Bay, at Florence, at Waldport, at Toledo, on the Siletz Bay, and at Hobsonville on Tillamook Bay. Florence and the lower Siuslaw were especially active areas. The first major cargo mill was the Saubert mill, built in 1884 at Acme on the Siuslaw Bay by Dr. William Saubert.[4] It reached an annual cut of one million board feet by 1902. A nearby mill at Florence had a capacity of 30 thousand board feet per day. This capacity would produce an annual cut of six million board feet, assuming a 200-day working year. The mill in Florence reported nearly eight million board feet for 1902, however, suggesting that they worked more than the 200 days.[5] The Siuslaw

Vessels loading lumber, C.A. Smith mill, North Bend. C.P. Cronk photo, 1910-1911.

Early mill at Waldport.

Lumber Company mill, also at Acme, cut over five million board feet between 1902 and 1905. Other small cargo mills in the central coast ports typically cut less than five million board feet most years, except for the mill at Hobsonville, on Tillamook Bay, which averaged around ten million board feet.

During the years that the Gardiner Mill Company was part of the lumber and shipping empire of Asa M. Simpson, it had access to Simpson's California marketing network and the Simpson fleet of ships. Other cargo mills were not as fortunate. The mills at Waldport depended on several small vessels that could navigate the Alsea River's shallow bar to enter or leave the bay. Some of these vessels were built on the Alsea. The *Lizzie*, for example, was built in 1872 at Tidewater and sailed around the Pacific until she wrecked on the Yaquina bar in 1876.[6] Another local schooner, the *W.H. Harrison*, was the largest of the fleet at 90 feet. She was owned by the Harrison Brothers Lumber Company in Waldport, successor firm to the Baldwin Lumber Company. After a short but disastrous career, the *Harrison* wrecked on the Alsea bar.

The bars of the Alsea and Siletz rivers are no longer considered navigable. Each winter small vessels are lost at the entrances of Coos Bay, Winchester Bay, the Siuslaw River, Yaquina Bay, and Tillamook Bay. During the years of the cargo trade small sturdy coastal ships made a precarious living by taking loads of lumber and log rafts out of these bays.

Crew on donkey engine. C.P. Cronk photo, 1910-1911.

RAILROAD MILLS

Boiler, cylinder, and winch on donkey engine.

The 1880s brought profound technological changes to the U.S. lumber industry. These included John Dolbeer's 1881 invention of the donkey engine, the development of railroad logging through the 1880s, and the use of band saws in mills after 1885.[7] The donkey engine was a steam-powered winch mounted on log skids. The winch cable could pull logs through the brush. With a high lead system, the donkey could move logs over stumps, rocks, and downed timber. The whole complex of skid roads, oxen, splash dams, and other expedients was rendered obsolete. Marjorie H. Hays notes that "Dolbeer's Patented Steam Donkey" made logging on the coast "seem like play compared to oxen and horses."[8]

Once the donkey engine had dragged or "yarded" the log out of the woods, another donkey engine could lift it onto a waiting rail car on the logging railroad. The railroad would whisk the logs to a bay, a river, or a mill pond, and they were ready for the saw. In Oregon, the Isthmus Transit Railroad, which was operating near Coos Bay in 1876, is generally accepted as the first logging railroad in the state.[9] Later logging railroads were built by other mills on the coast, in the Willamette Valley, on the Columbia, and in the eastern Oregon pine country. By 1906, at least 30 lumber companies in Oregon were operating logging railroads, including the Gardiner Mill Company.

The final step in the mechanization of the lumber industry was getting the sawmill hooked up to the transcontinental railroad system. When this connection was achieved,

U.S. plywood mill, Mapleton, 1950s.

Manary Logging Company train, 1920s. Lloyd Palmer collection.

a boxcar could be loaded with lumber in Toledo, Oregon, for example, and sold to a customer in Trenton, New Jersey. The old Oregon Pacific Railroad and branch lines of the Southern Pacific brought rail service into the coast country. The Oregon Pacific was the first to reach the coast, connecting Yaquina Bay to the Willamette Valley in 1885. A branch of the Southern Pacific reached Tillamook Bay in 1911. The Southern Pacific built a branch line west to Cushman, then south through Gardiner to Coos Bay in 1916. With the railroad connection, mills on the coast no longer needed to depend on selling lumber to the local market or on the hazards of maritime shipping.

The largest railroad mill adjacent to the Siuslaw was the huge mill and remanufacturing plant built by the U.S. Army's Spruce Production Division at Toledo. This mill and the railroad that served it were capable of producing 600 thousand board feet (MBF) of lumber per day. The Gardiner mill, which was served by the Southern Pacific Railroad after 1916, could cut 100 MBF per day. On Tillamook Bay, the A.F. Coats Lumber Company mill also had a 100 MBF capacity. Three mills near Reedsport cut between 100 and 150 MBF, making Winchester Bay one of the major industrial areas on the coast. Other railroad mills adjacent to the Siuslaw were considerably smaller, with daily production between 30 and 50 MBF.

One of the pioneer railroad mills on the coast was the Fir and Spruce Lumber Company. The firm incorporated in Toledo, on the Oregon Pacific Railroad, in 1906.[10]

In 1907 the company began building a logging railroad from Depot Slough north to their timber land on the Siletz River. They acquired at least four donkey engines, a locomotive, and increased the capacity of their mill to 75 thousand board feet per day. During the next 15 years, the mill changed ownership and name numerous times. Loggers cut timber on Depot Slough and Ollala Slough, on the Yaquina River, and along the company's railroad as it was built north toward the town of Siletz. Finally, in 1923, Pacific Spruce bought the railroad, and the mill passed into the hands of the Creamery Package Manufacturing Company, which made spruce boxes and tubs for dairies until 1944. The logging railroad, under the ownership of Pacific Spruce and later Georgia Pacific, eventually reached Logsden before it was abandoned in the 1950s.

Loggers in camp. C.P. Cronk photo, 1910-1911.

On the Siuslaw River, the Southern Pacific ran west along the river to Cushman, near the eastern end of the bay, then crossed to the south side of the river and ran south to the Coos Bay area. The town of Florence was not served by the railroad. In 1919, the logging firm of Vaughan and Bester began a logging railroad on Bernhardt Creek (also called Lawson Creek) on the south bank of the Siuslaw River.[11] This drainage was "alienated" or private land within the Siuslaw National Forest. This drainage was not served by the Southern Pacific, so Vaughan and Bester had to move their locomotive, cars, and rails across the river by barge before they could begin operations. Logs cut on the Bernhardt Creek drainage were dumped in the river and towed to a point where they were loaded onto Southern Pacific rail cars for delivery to the mills at Coos Bay.

Crib trestling.

In 1920, Vaughan and Bester bought the old Saubert mill at Acme (now Cushman). They built a second logging

Vaughan and Bester Lumber Company Heisler locomotive. Lloyd Palmer collection.

camp and railroad on Hadsall Creek near Mapleton. Again, they were logging on the south side of the Siuslaw River on private land adjacent to the Siuslaw National Forest. The two railroads and the mill at Cushman continued to produce lumber through the 1920s, albeit with some financial vicissitudes and several new owners. The operation finally fell victim to the Depression in 1929.[12]

Other small railroad logging operations on the lower Siuslaw included the Delta Shingle Company, with a railroad up Morris Creek on the North Fork of the Siuslaw. Crown Timber of Mapleton operated a short railroad up Knowles Creek. L.C. Reynolds operated a railroad on Karnowsky Creek. Gid Ross operated a railroad on Wendson Creek, and an unknown logging firm operated a railroad on Hoffman Creek.[13] Each of these railroads was "landlocked" in that there was no connection to any other railroad. The locomotive, cars, and rails had to be hauled laboriously overland to the starting point, then the railroad was built from that point into the timber. Once the railroad was operating, it brought logs out of the woods. They were dumped into the river and rafted down to the mill.

For the most part, these mills relied on private timber land to supply their logs. The one exception is the Delta Shingle Company, which bought cedar sales from the Siuslaw National Forest as early as 1915.[14] The 1915 sale was for 200,000 board feet of cedar. Delta bought over four million feet in 1920, and 200,000 feet in 1921. Cedar, of course, did not grow in pure stands, so a cedar mill had to get logs wherever it could, often from other logging companies as an incidental product cut in their fir operations.

The largest lumber operation on the central Oregon coast was the Pacific Spruce Company mill at Toledo, with logging railroads south to the Blodgett Tract and north to the Siletz River. Like other central coast mills before World War II, Pacific Spruce cut mostly private timber. However, since its largest timber holdings are now a part of the Siuslaw National Forest, and these lands were owned by a subsidiary of the U.S. government when Pacific Spruce logged them in the 1920s, we can consider that Pacific Spruce was cutting public timber.

Large Sitka spruce log. SPD photo, ca. 1918.

After World War I ended on November 11, 1918, the Army transferred its Spruce Production Division (SPD) to a government corporation, the Spruce Production Corporation (SPC). This organization set about selling all the SPD assets, including millions of dollars worth of donkey engines, locomotives, mill, and logging equipment. The volume of mill and logging equipment sold by the SPC was so great that it supplied the entire West Coast industry for years. The SPC also put the unfinished mill at Toledo, the logging railroads built to supply the mill, and the 12,705 acre Blodgett Tract up for sale. A second SPD property at Port Angeles, Washington, including a mill, some timber, and railroads, was also offered for sale.

Spruce logs on SPD train. SPD photo, ca. 1918.

Donkey engine at Manary Camp, Oregon.

The SPD properties eventually sold, and the buyers in both cases were groups of investors assembled by San Francisco entrepreneur Fentress Hill. Fentress Hill, with F.S. Scritsmeir of Portland, R.J. Dunham of Chicago, and Wendell Kuhn of Portland formed the Pacific Spruce Corporation to buy the Toledo properties in 1920. Later, Hill, John K. Lyon, and F.S. Scritsmeir created a second firm—Lyon, Hill and Company—to buy the Port Angeles properties in 1922. Hill had been manager of Lyon, Gary and Company, a financial firm in Chicago. Corporate officers in Lyon, Gary and Company included Calvin Fentress and Lucius Baker, who were in turn involved in Baker, Fentress and Company of Chicago. Baker, Fentress was one of the largest financial firms lending money to the lumber business.

In January of 1918, Hill had attempted to buy the old-growth spruce forest on the Blodgett Tract from John Blodgett. Hill wrote in a letter to Blodgett on January 2, 1918, that he was interested in the tract so that he could "open it up" and make the spruce available to the war effort.[15] Blodgett refused to sell to Hill, and the SPD eventually purchased the tract. Hill led his associates into the spruce business in the early 1920s and then led them out of it. In 1924, the Hill group sold most of the Pacific Spruce Corporation to Southern lumberman C.D. Johnson.[16] In 1927, they sold the Port Angeles properties as well.

Timber on the Blodgett Tract.

C.D. Johnson had been a successful lumberman in Louisiana, but he had sold his mills and lands as the southern pine industry began to contract. The industry periodicals advised that the future of lumber lay "out West" so businessmen from the Great Lakes and the South moved into the Pacific states.

Johnson set up four separate corporations to handle the new business. Pacific Spruce Corporation managed the mill at Toledo from its offices in Portland. The Manary Logging Company managed the logging and the Alsea Southern Railway. C.D. Johnson Lumber Company sold the lumber that the mill produced. To balance his spruce timber on the Blodgett Tract, Johnson bought 14,626 acres of timber on the Siletz River, largely Douglas fir. To reach the Siletz timber, he bought the old Fir and Spruce Lumber Company railroad, which ran up Depot Slough to the Siletz. He incorporated this fourth business as the Pacific Spruce Northern Railway.

Manary Logging, under the supervision of veteran logger James Manary, repaired the railroad from South Beach to Waldport in the spring of 1922. Camp Two, 12 miles south of South Beach, began cutting logs in the summer of 1922. Camp One, south of Waldport, opened in the fall. Spur one, on the Blodgett Tract, was delivering logs by this time. During the next few years, additional spurs were built to reach all through the Blodgett Tract.[17]

Large trestle with vertical bents.

Logging technology on the Manary Logging Company "show" was state-of-the-art. The system was typical of the sophisticated steam-powered systems developed in the Coast Range and on the west slope of the Cascades in the Pacific Northwest. Lumber industry publicists B.A. Johnson and Archibald Whisnat described the system as a "swing" system in their promotional material about the company. The system began when loggers topped and guyed a head spar tree near the railroad spur. At the base of the spar, a huge donkey engine—the head spar donkey—pulled a two inch steel cable—the skyline—out to a tail spar tree, which was also topped and guyed. A tail spar donkey moved out to the base of the tail spar, and loggers set the high lead lines and the haulback cables from the top of the tail spar.

In operation, loggers felled trees and bucked them into logs within a 1000 foot radius of the tail spar. The logs were hooked to the high lead line and the tail spar donkey winched them in to the base of the tail spar. Then the logs were hooked to the sky line with one end suspended off the ground. The head spar donkey then winched them to a

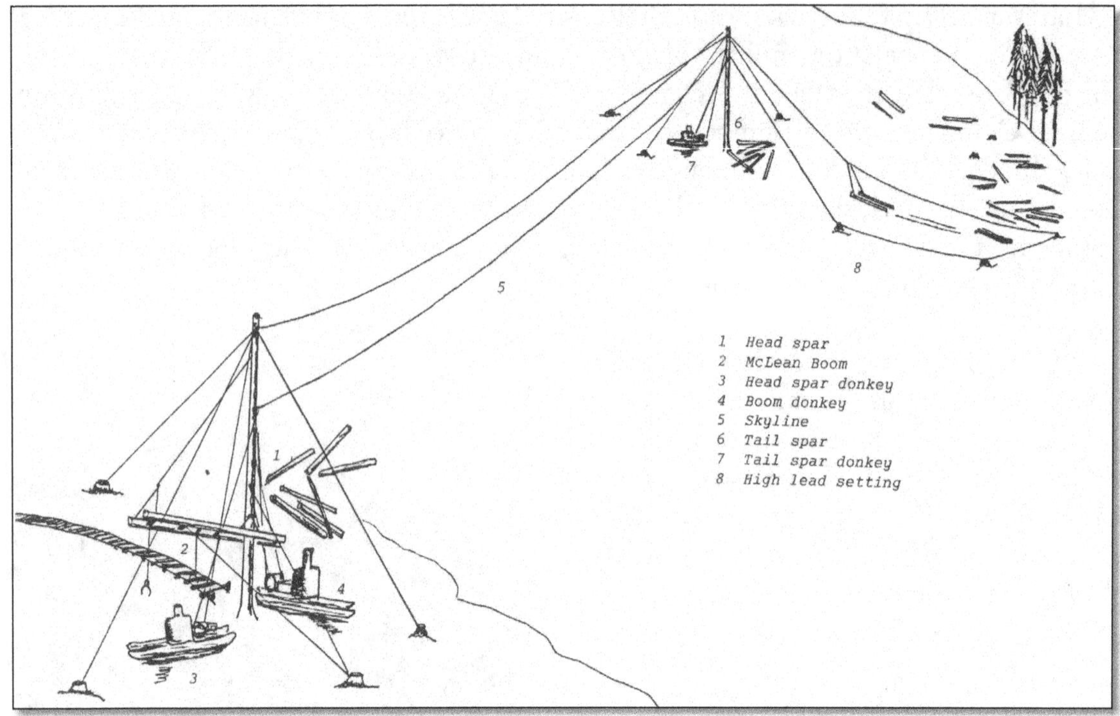

Diagram of high-lead logging system used by Manary Logging Company.

pile—or deck—at the base of the head spar. When the logging locomotive brought up the empty cars, a third donkey engine loaded the logs onto the rail cars for the trip to the mill.

When all the logs within a 1,000 foot radius of the tail spar had been cut, the loggers selected another tail spar tree, and the process began again. When all logs tributary to the head spar had been cut and yarded out, the loggers chose a new head spar further along the rail spur. This logging system was complicated but very productive. As much as five million board feet of timber could be yarded out from one head spar setting. At the turn of the century—23 years earlier—only three or four mills on the coast could have cut five million board feet in a full year's operation.[18]

On the timber lands north of Toledo on the Siletz River, the Manary Logging Company operated Camp 11 and Camp 12. Camp 12 was served by the Pacific Spruce Northern railroad which delivered logs to the mill. The logging operation at Camp 12 was similar to the one at Camp One. Camp 11, however, was not on the railroad. It was further north on the Siletz River. Loggers located their head spars close to the river and dumped the full-length logs into the water. A tow boat then moved the logs downriver to booming grounds, where they were assembled into rafts. These were towed out to sea over the Siletz bar and delivered to the mill at Toledo. Loggers lived in a large houseboat on the river.

I had a friend who was a Steam shovel
operator who talked the Manary logging Co into a
contract to building grade for $1.00 a foot (lineal)
This man (Jack Lommas) by name bought a
new (Logger Special Erie Shovel) and I went to
work for him in September 1925
we built a spur up Big Creek and finished
I before Xmas. Our next spur was on
spur 5. This spur we worked on untill
the next may. This was all the grade
Jack built at Camp one and we went to
Camp 12 and built 2 or 3 spurs for
Manary logging Co.

Letter from Ron Hadley describing construction of Manary Logging Company railroad spurs, 1982.

THE PACIFIC SPRUCE CORPORATION MILL

Spruce lumber dries in yard, Pacific Spruce Corporation Mill in Toledo.

The unfinished mill that Pacific Spruce bought from the Army at Toledo was designed to cut airplane spruce. Pacific Spruce redesigned the mill to cut different lumber products and equipped it with new machinery. Like most lumber mills of its time, the Toledo mill burned wood waste, bark, and sawdust to fire the boilers. Steam from the boilers ran turbines which made electricity, heated the dry kiln, and operated some steam-powered machinery like the head-rig carriage. The 3,200 kilowatt turbine generator produced enough electricity to run the mill's machinery and deliver excess electricity to the towns of Newport and Toledo.

Pacific Spruce combined aspects of a railroad mill with aspects of a cargo mill. Most of the firm's lumber was shipped by rail to U.S. destinations. The company also owned the *Robert S. Johnson*, a cargo ship that delivered lumber to California ports. The *Robert S. Johnson* carried box lumber and lath to California each month at the rate of three million board feet per voyage.[19]

Like other mills, Pacific Spruce attempted to make as many finished lumber products as possible. These were more valuable than the lumber itself. Products listed by Pacific Spruce included fir flooring, fir ladder stock, California novelty siding, spruce bevel siding, and high-grade spruce and fir for shop and factory use. The mill produced spruce box lumber (called "shook") and spruce lath. The mill also produced framing lumber, shelving, and dozens of other construction-grade products. Flooring, ladder stock, and high-grade lumber were valuable; construction lumber and siding were less valuable, and box shook and lath were low value items.

[Sitka spruce] does not warp or split and therefore is particularly adapted for core stock for veneered articles....It is also well adapted for many other purposes, such as refrigerator stock, sash and doors, ladder stock, car stock, framing, shelving, sheathing, flooring, lath, ceiling, stepping, siding, battens, turning squares, moulding lumber, moulding, factory lumber, panel stock, car siding and roofing, common dimension, in fact, Sitka spruce is an excellent wood where such qualities as ease of working and painting, light weight, and ability to take and hold nails are required.

B.A. Johnson and Archie Whisnat, *Pacific Spruce Corporation*

Pacific Spruce faced a declining market for spruce. Aircraft production had driven the price of Sitka spruce up during World War I, but aircraft makers were switching to aluminum, and the market for aircraft spruce was gone. Johnson and Whisnat devoted considerable energy in their promotional material on the uses of spruce lumber. Their point was that spruce was a good substitute for fir or poplar as finish lumber, and was good for veneer base, boxes, cooperage, and musical instruments.

The apogee of Pacific Spruce's fortune came in 1925. The national market for lumber of all kinds was strong, and Pacific Spruce was cutting about 500 thousand board feet each day. In September of 1925, the firm sold and shipped more than 15 million board feet of lumber, 70 percent of which was Douglas fir.[20] Pacific Spruce began to experience financial problems soon after. The Manary Logging Company operation was bankrupt and dismantled in 1927. The company sold assets including the tugs and barges in 1928. By 1930 Pacific Spruce was in receivership. The company was broken up in 1934 and shorn of its railroads and steamship. The remaining assets were sold to C.D. Johnson, and it emerged from bankruptcy as the C.D. Johnson Lumber Company.[21]

One asset that Pacific Spruce could not lose was the Blodgett Tract because it had never owned it. The sales contract that Johnson had arranged with the Spruce Production Corporation left the land in the name of the SPC until Pacific Spruce had paid the purchase price. Pacific Spruce made a $50,000 down payment and paid for timber cut at a fixed price per thousand board feet, but did not complete the sale of the real property.[22] Accordingly, the Tract remained in the hands of the Spruce Production Corporation.

What the government held was no prize, however. Manary's highly mechanized logging had a significant impact on the land. Colonel Brice P. Disque and his advisors had advocated selective logging on the Tract because of the over-mature timber and the mix of species. The system Manary employed could not be used for selective logging. Worse, the high speed of the yarders—over 500 feet of cable per minute—killed 50 to 90 percent of the young trees under 3.5 inches in diameter.[23] Manary logged in a hurry, so slash and cull timber was not burned, and it littered the ground. In 1936, 10,000 cut-over acres of the Tract burned in a major forest fire. The Siuslaw National Forest bought the Tract as the Yaquina Purchase Unit in 1941. C.D. Johnson died in 1940, and Georgia Pacific bought his company in the 1950s.

[Manary Logging] took only the clear logs, so the waste was terrible. All the debris was left on the ground—it was a mess.

Forest Supervisor Rex Wakefield Interview, 1980

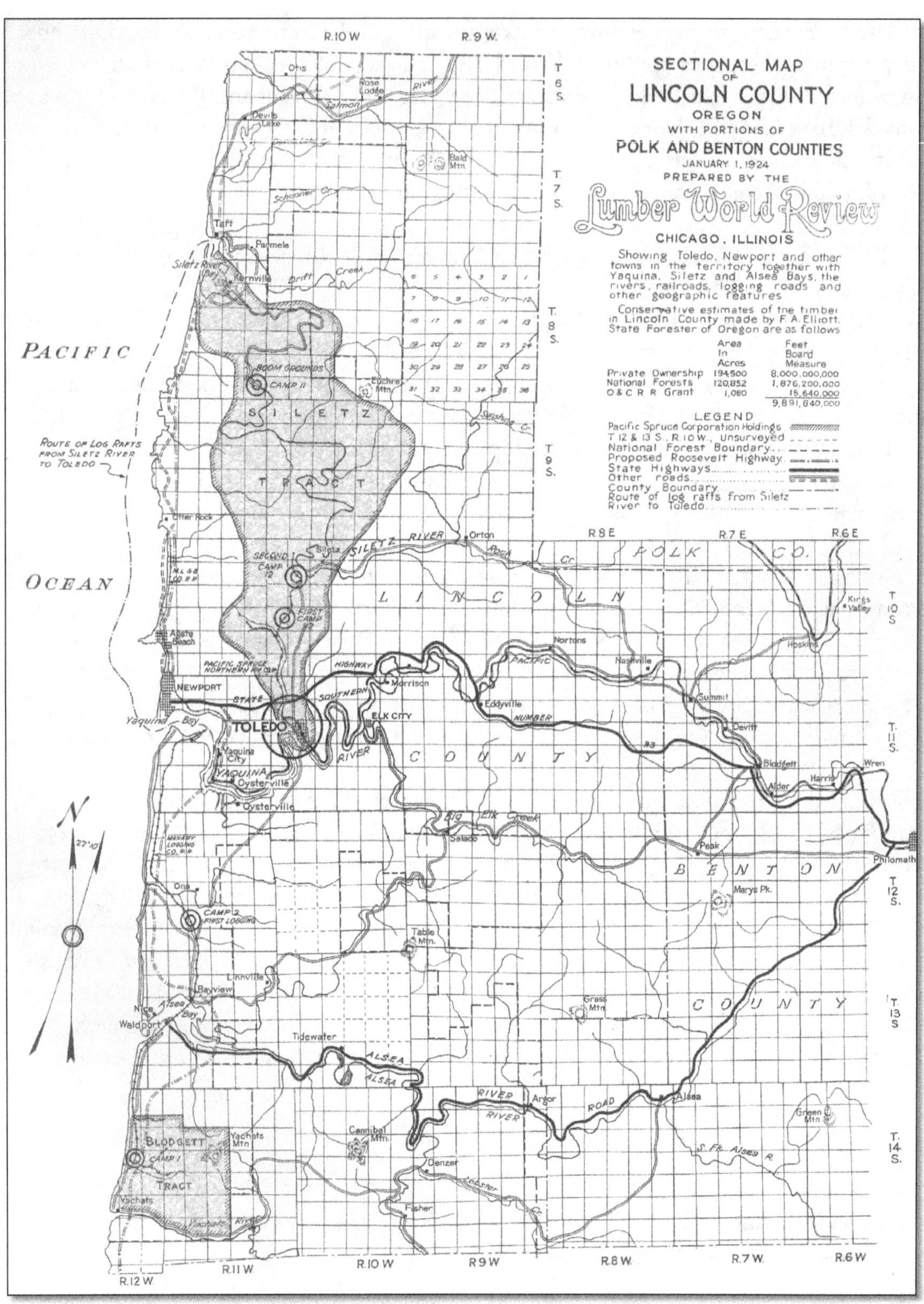

Map of Pacific Spruce Corporation timber lands from Johnson and Whisnat.

WORLD WAR II AND AFTER

During World War II, the pace of timber sales on the Siuslaw increased. The Forest sold 153.5 million board feet during 1942-1945. This was more than the total sales from 1915 through 1941. The demand for lumber to support the war effort spurred sales, and lumber companies that survived the Depression were eager to make up for their financial reverses. Internal combustion logging technology began to replace steam technology during the late 1930s and 1940s. Advertisements for motor trucks, diesel tractors, diesel yarders, and gasoline-powered chain saws appeared in industry periodicals during these years. Trucks and tractors were comparatively inexpensive and enabled smaller logging operators to get into the business. The large mills like Pacific Spruce had trouble finding capital to keep up their railroad systems, or employ the large workforce required by steam logging.

During the War, the Siuslaw was divided into the Hebo Ranger District, the Waldport Ranger District, the Gardiner Ranger District, and the Mapleton Ranger District. Each district increased its number of sales. On the Hebo Ranger District, for example, three large sales were active in 1942 and 1943. These were the Jewell Creek sale, the Squaw Creek sale, and the Sourgrass Summit sale. Coats Lumber Company of Tillamook bought the Jewell Creek sale. The other two sales went to smaller operators. Annual cut on Hebo at that time was four to six million board feet.[24]

Davidson Mill, Mapleton, 1950s.

Logging on the wartime Hebo Ranger District sales was done by truck. Conscientious objectors stationed at Cedar Creek spike camp replanted after the sales were harvested. Sales conducted prior to 1945 did not include road building within the contracts. After 1946, however, road building was part of the contract on Hebo sales. Later, some contracts required clearcutting. In ten years between 1943 and 1953, the allowable cut on the Hebo Ranger District rose from 4-6 million board feet to 52 million. Total cut on the Siuslaw was 113.6 million board feet in 1953. During 1954, there were 31 advertised sales on Hebo and 46 unadvertised sales.[25]

THE BIG CUT: 1960s, 1970s AND 1980s

One of the last steam yarders decking logs, 1960s.

Beginning in 1958, the Siuslaw sold over 300 million board feet of timber each year. This level of sales was sustained for 33 years through the 1960s, 1970s, and 1980s. The Siuslaw's years of increased productivity coincided with similar increases on other national forests in Oregon and Washington, especially on the Umpqua, the Willamette, the Olympic, and the Mt. Hood. There were various reasons for the huge harvest in the Northwest during these years. National demand for lumber was increasing. Many lumber companies had cut or liquidated their timber during the Depression and World War II, so they had to rely on public timber sales. And, on a nationwide basis, the timber lands of the Great Lakes, the Mid-Atlantic, and the South were exhausted.

Heel boom loader at work.

With the increased volume of timber and the increased number of sales, there was a corresponding increase in the work of sales administration. The Forest Service needed to plan sales, cruise the timber, mark and map the sales, administer the contracts, and monitor the logging. This required more personnel on each ranger district. The increasing number of personnel threatened the close, family culture that had prevailed throughout the organization.

Logging technology during the 1960s and 1970s changed a little, but remained wedded to the cable logging systems developed in the 1910s and 1920s. Skidding logs

> **It may have been in 1957 or early 1958 that an industry organization was putting pressure on us to raise our annual cut by doing partial cutting. But I do not recall that we made any partial cut sales, except small ones to pick up beetle-kill and windfalls.**
>
> **Clarence W. Jacobs, *Working for the U.S. Forest Service***

Large log in the 1950s.

by caterpillar tractor was not much practiced on the steep slopes and fragile soils of the Siuslaw. Cable yarding permitted loggers to work effectively on the steepest slopes. In addition to the older high-lead systems, there were more complicated skyline systems. During the 1950s many of the steam-powered donkey engines were replaced by gasoline or diesel yarders.

Heel boom loader decking logs, Mapleton sale.

In the 1960s, donkey engines and spar trees were replaced by steel-tower yarders that had the winches and the steel spar mounted together on a chassis with either wheels or tracks. Loading logs with a spar tree and a McClean boom gave way to self-propelled loaders, often adapted from excavating equipment and mounted on either wheels or tracks. Lloyd Palmer, a retired timber sale manager from the Waldport Ranger District, recalls that the 1971 Howell sale was the last time he saw a spar tree used. After the courts stopped road-building in the Mapleton District in 1984, swing yarding was briefly resumed by loggers who had to remove timber without using motor vehicles.[26]

The chain saw was another technological development of the post-World War II period. This technology had been in use since early in the century, especially in Europe. Loggers in the U.S. and Canada did not easily relinquish their crosscut saws, however.

The major effort during the year [1963] was the preparation and sale of over 637,000,000 board feet of timber at a value of $15 million. This is twice the regular yearly accomplishment.

Siuslaw National Forest "Historical Notes for 1963"

"Jake Mann was the first logger to buy an SJ-4 mobile yarder-loader."

Clarence W. Jacobs, *Working for the U.S. Forest Service*

Early chain saws in the 1940s were heavy and unreliable. Worse, there was no common technology. Saws could be driven by two-stroke engines, four-stroke engines, or electric motors powered by generators mounted on tractors. Chains were difficult to maintain. Saws had to be used in a upright position, so the operator had to rotate the bar and chain mechanism to make felling cuts. By the 1950s, however, chain saws were replacing crosscuts as a new generation of loggers took over.[27]

Clearcut logging, which removed all trees of all ages and conditions from a sale area, was a feature of sales in the 1950s and 1960s, and soon became controversial. Public groups opposed to clearcutting in the Rocky Mountains and in the Pacific Northwest were vociferous in their complaints. As a result, the Forest Service began to include provisions for public comment to proposed sales and timber management programs. As Forest Service historian Gerald Williams points out, the clearcutting controversy of the 1960s and 1970s led Congress to pass the National Forest Management Act of 1976.[28]

Through the 1980s mill and logging technology was changing in the West. Yarders designed for large, old-growth trees were replaced with smaller yarders designed for smaller, second growth trees. On some sales, feller-bunchers and timber forwarders replaced yarders altogether. In some especially sensitive areas, logging by helicopter was required. Mills responded to the changing log size by installing small log equipment that could cut smaller logs more efficiently.

Russ Hollowell cuts spruce from springboard, 1970. Loyd Collet photo.

Mills processing timber from the Siuslaw during the 1960s, 1970s, and 1980s included the large mills at Toledo, operated by Georgia Pacific, and at Gardiner, operated by Long-Bell and International Paper. Other smaller mills were located on the Alsea, at Mapleton, at Five Rivers, at Lobster Creek, and at Tillamook. Many sales of Siuslaw timber went to the mills in the Willamette Valley. The highway development that began in the 1930s and continued through later decades made long-distance hauling of logs economically expedient.

BH: Tell us a little of what timber cruising was like at that time.

DB: Well, back then we pretty much found the units for the areas that we wanted to log, and we were logging old-growth. We flagged the boundaries and then go in and cruise the timber. There were different methods. A lot of it was 100 percent. We'd go in and pretty much measure every tree. Then there were some other methods where we would measure every tenth tree and do some plots. Go with two chains and measure every tree within a plot.

BH: So you were basically clear-cutting?

DB: We were clear-cutting, yeah. It was, back then it was all clear-cutting.

Dave Beck Interview, 2005 with Barbara Henderson

The demand for raw materials as related to the annual allowable cut has caused concern. Although a certain portion of the timber supply must come from private land, several developments are planned for the Forest to help narrow the gap between supply and demand. The field work for reinventory has been completed which should indicate an upward revision of the allowable cut. Salvage sales have kept cutting well over the allowable cut, but this alone will not meet the demand for timber. Priorities of management to help needs are through salvage of diseased or dead timber, conversion of low-producing areas, and thinning young stands.

Siuslaw National Forest "Historical Notes for 1956"

Workers pulling lumber on the "green chain."

Timber sales during the 1980s included fewer large old-growth trees. As the big slower yarders wore out they were replaced with slightly smaller, faster ones with a focus on second growth timber harvests.

North Fork Siuslaw Watershed Plan, 1995

Before 1980, most mills stored their logs in rivers, bays, or ponds. This practice kept the logs moist and made them easy to handle. Log trucks delivered logs "down to splash," and the bull chains of the mill pulled logs out of the water as they were needed. In 1980, however, the newly-formed Oregon Department of Environmental Quality created

Unloading log truck.

Logs stored on the Siuslaw River.

regulations that would phase out water storage of logs. Logs in rivers and bays were found to release tannins that could harm fish and wildlife.

Road building in the forest was critical to logging during the 1960s, 1970s, and 1980s. Logging companies built roads as part of their contracts with the Siuslaw. At the end of the sale, most roads remained in use for future logging or for recreational visitors. The roads had an impact on wildlife and increased the danger of human-caused fires. Some poorly designed roads also affected the watershed, concentrating water run-off, creating drainage problems, and causing landslides.

As wildlife needs were recognized, the large 80 to 120 acre clearcuts were reduced to less than 60 acres and later to less than 40 acres. Woody debris and standing snags and trees were retained.

North Fork Siuslaw Watershed Analysis, 1994

In the 1990s environmental legislation and the Northwest Forest Plan brought the years of heavy cutting to an end. Timber volume on the Siuslaw fell from 381.7 million board feet in 1990 to 12.4 million in 1991. In recent years, timber volume has stabilized at around 30 million board feet. Most of the volume is smaller trees that are selectively cut within stands less than 80 years old. These are expected to become late-succession forests in the future.

Fiscal Year	*Volume in MMBF Sold	Harvested
FY 80	384.9	266.6
FY 81	406.6	247.4
FY 82	367.4	142.1
FY 83	369.6	242.8
FY 84	289.7	338.9
FY 85	278.4	305.2
FY 86	346.0	312.0
FY 87	365.2	361.5
FY 88	346.3	420.8
FY 89	254.9	297.7
FY 90	381.7	171.0
FY 91	12.4	149.5
FY 92	4.2	100.7
FY 93	2.5	32.3
FY 94	4.6	15.2
FY 95	9.2	23.8
FY 96	28.2	21.0
FY 97	28.7	5.0
FY 98	3.0	28.2
FY 99	11.4	15.9
FY 2000	2.2	20.1
FY 01	1.9	9.7
FY 02	24.9	8.4
FY 03	35.5	20.1
FY 04	22.8	16.5
FY 05	26.3	17.8
FY 06	25.2	24.8

**Volumes are in million board feet (MMBF) and include convertible forest products.*

Helicopter logging was used in some sales during the 1970s. Loyd Collett photo.

Log stacker unloads logs.

NORTH FORK SIUSLAW WATERSHED

GROWTH OF ROAD SYSTEM THRU TIME

*DATES REPRESENT SYSTEM ROADS BUILT UP TO THAT TIME

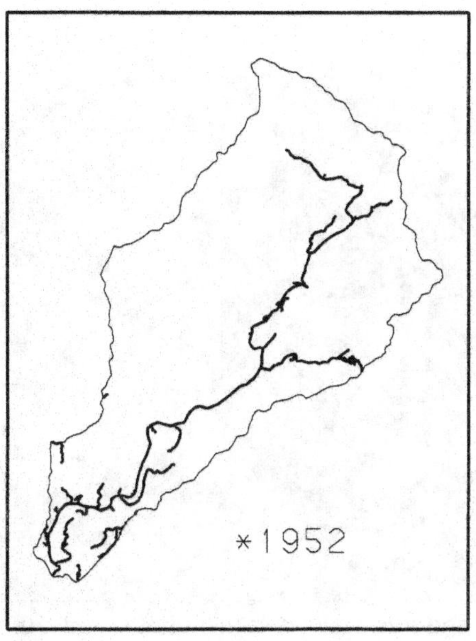

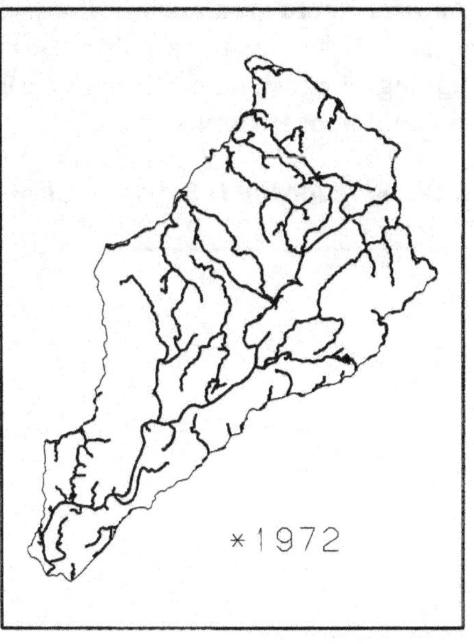

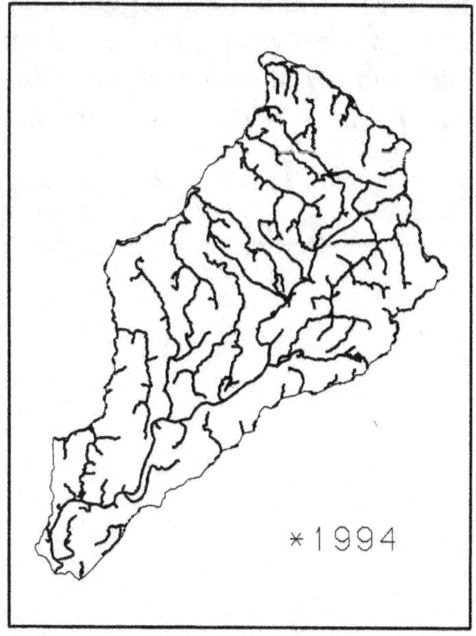

Landing scene showing steel-tower yarder, loader, and trucks. Lloyd Palmer photo, ca. 1970s.

When there was a lot of logging activity in an area there was always danger of meeting a heavily loaded log truck coming down a narrow road from a high ridge...I would stop my pickup and listen for the coughing of a big diesel truck coming down...A wise trucker would send out an occasional hoot with the loud air horn.

Clarence W. Jacobs, *Working for the U.S. Forest Service*

NOTES

1 *Siuslaw National Forest Lands Classification Atlas* (on file, Waldport, OR: Siuslaw NF, 1919) 5.

2 For a discussion of early sawmills, see Stephen D. Beckham, *History of the Siuslaw National Forest* (on file, Waldport, OR: Siuslaw NF, 1982) 255-261 and David Fagan, *History of Benton County* (Portland, OR: A.G. Walling, 1885)

3 Beckham, 258-259, figures from *The Timberman.*

4 Lloyd Palmer, "Logging Railroads Along the Lower Siuslaw" (on file, Waldport, OR: Siuslaw NF, 2001).

5 Beckham, 258.

6 Marjorie H. Hays, *The Land That Kept its Promise* (Newport, OR: Lincoln County Historical Society, 1976) 64.

7 Ward Tonsfeldt, "Railroad Logging in Oregon" (on file, Salem, OR: Oregon State Historic Preservation Office, 1993) 22-33.

8 Hays, 77.

9 John T. Labbe, "The Isthmus Transit Railroad," *Narrow Gauge and Shortline Gazette*, September 1988, 17-21.

10 For a good discussion of the complex history of this mill, see Lloyd Palmer, "The Other Toledo Sawmill" (on file, Waldport, OR: Siuslaw NF, 2005).

11 See Lloyd Palmer, "Logging Railroads Along the Lower Siuslaw River," for a complete discussion of the Vaughan and Bester railroad logging operations.

12 Palmer 2001.

13 Palmer 2001.

14 Palmer 2001.

15 Blodgett Papers, University of Minnesota Special Collections; Hill to Blodgett, January 2, 1918.

16 Lloyd Palmer, *Steam Towards the Sunset* (Newport, OR: Lincoln County Historical Society, 1982) 162.

17 B.A. Johnson and A. Whisnat, *Pacific Spruce Corporation* (Chicago, IL: Lumber World Review, 1924) 36-38.

18 Details of the Manary swing system are available in Johnson and Whisnat, 38.

19 Johnson and Whisnat, 73.

20 *The Timberman*, October 1925, 6.

21 Palmer 1982, 165.

22 Stephanie Finucane, *A History of the Blodgett Tract* (Corvallis, OR: Siuslaw NF, 1980) 18.

23 Nelson C. Brown, *Logging: the Principles and Practice of Harvesting Timber in the United States and Canada* (New York, NY: John Wiley, 1934) 189.

24 Rolfe Anderson, "Hebo District Historical Notes, 1907-1966" (on file, Waldport, OR: Siuslaw NF, n.d.).

25 Anderson.

26 Comments by retired forester Don Large.

27 See David Lee, *Chainsaws, A History* (Vancouver BC: Harbour Publishing, 2006).

28 Gerald W. Williams, *The USDA Forest Service—The First Century* (Washington, DC: USDA Forest Service, 2000) 113-116.

CHAPTER SEVEN

RECREATION

THE BEGINNINGS OF RECREATION ON THE NATIONAL FORESTS

When Gifford Pinchot—first Chief Forester—wrote *The Use of the National Forests* in 1907, he had some ideas about recreation, but his thinking was not fully formulated. He mentions that "stores, hotels, and residences for recreation" belonged on the national forests because they contributed to "getting the fullest use out of the land and its resources."[1]

Cape Perpetua was one of the first sites on the Siuslaw set aside for recreation.

***Playgrounds.* Quite incidentally, also, the national forests serve a good purpose as great playgrounds for the people. They are used more or less every year by campers, hunters, fishermen, and thousands of pleasure seekers from the near-by towns. They are great recreation grounds for a very large part of the people of the West, and their value in this respect is well worth considering.**

Gifford Pinchot, *The Use of the National Forests*

While Pinchot was not willing to include recreation as a fundamental purpose of the new national forests he was willing to consider its role. At a personal level, Pinchot was enthusiastic about outdoor recreation, especially yachting. His political mentor Teddy Roosevelt was a great believer in strenuous outdoor activities, and wrote books about his own adventures hunting and camping. It is probably fair to say that men like Pinchot and Roosevelt saw recreation and leisure as belonging to the wealthy classes with money and time to pursue them.

Trail shelters were used by Forest Service staff and by the recreating public.

In the early days Forest Service policy followed Pinchot's thinking and treated recreation as less important than other more traditional uses of the forests. However, there was opposition to this view from inside and outside the Forest Service. Conservationists like California's John Muir and Oregon's John B. Waldo had been among the first advocates of the forest reserve and national forest programs. They argued that the national forests should be used for "inspiration and our own true recreation," and not for grazing, mining, or timber. Men like Muir reached a large national audience with their writings and influenced national policy. Within the Forest Service early advocates of recreation included Arthur Carhart, Aldo Leopold, Fred Waugh, and Fred Cleator.

Pinchot's successor as Chief Forester was Henry S. Graves, who took a different view of forest recreation in his 1913 *Annual Report of the Forester.*

> *[Recreation] is a highly important use of the Forests by the public, and it is recognized and facilitated by adjusting commercial use of the Forests, when necessary. Examples are the exclusion of stock and provisions in timber sales for very light cutting, or not cutting at all close to lakes and elsewhere where it is desirable to preserve the natural beauty of the location unmarred, for the enjoyment of the public.*
>
> Henry S. Graves *Annual Report of the Forester, 1913*

Forest recreation was probably attractive to Graves and other leaders of the Forest Service for practical reasons as well as for its own merit. Recreation was a non-consumptive use of the forest that could bring urban Americans into the national forests and show them the benefits of Forest Service management. This could create a new constituency of supporters who could balance the rural people and the industrialists who opposed federal forest management. For urban Americans of moderate means, forest recreation was very appealing—inexpensive, family oriented, and increasingly fashionable.

Early camping equipment, with reflector oven for baking. C.P. Cronk photo, 1910-1911.

In 1915, Congress passed the Term Occupancy Act on March 4. This legislation authorized the Secretary of Agriculture to issue special use permits on "suitable areas of land within the national forests, not exceeding five acres and for periods not exceeding thirty years, for the purpose of constructing and maintaining summer homes." Hotels, stores, and resorts were also approved uses of the permit lands.

In the same year, the Forest Service created the Columbia River Gorge Park on the Oregon National Forest (now the Mt. Hood NF). This park encompassed nearly 14,000 acres. Within the park was the Eagle Creek campground, the first developed campground on any national forest. The Eagle Creek hiking trail was a recreational trail over 13 miles long that afforded spectacular views of the Columbia Gorge. This complex was the most ambitious national forest recreation facility to date.[2] In the following year, 1916, Congress created the National Park Service within the Department of the Interior to manage the parks that were growing in popularity and becoming national oases for recreation. In 1917, The Forest Service engaged landscape architect Fred Waugh to investigate forest recreation. His report, *Recreational Uses of the National Forests*, was the first agency-wide approach to this topic. Three years later, Waugh prepared a report on the Mt. Hood area.

[On the Crater National Forest] we surveyed out a resort site called Rocky Point and 30 more summer home sites. By 1913 these were all sold and we surveyed and set aside 50 or more at Lake O'Woods. So far as I know, this was about the first attempt in the Region to recognize and develop recreational facilities.

Ranger Edward S. Kerby, 1924

EARLY RECREATION ON THE SIUSLAW

By virtue of its coastal location, the Siuslaw National Forest had a head start on recreation. It was located close to the populous Willamette Valley, offering convenient access for many Oregonians.

Coastal resorts in Lincoln and Tillamook counties advertised the appeal of the central Oregon beaches. Nye Beach near Newport was an early destination for "summer people" visiting the coast. At the turn of the century, Newport offered hotels, campgrounds, and even some claim to gentility.[3]

> **Socially Newport cannot be surpassed either in character of her visitors or class of her entertainments and amusements. She is free of all that objectionable class of people who crowd the resorts close to a large city.**
>
> **Vacation Suggestions, Yaquina Bay, 1898**

Coast access on the Siuslaw at the time included an area near Sand Lake in Tillamook County, Cape Perpetua, the South Lincoln County beaches, and the dunes from Florence south to Coos Bay. Before the Oregon Coast Highway was completed in the 1930s, access to the beaches on the Forest was difficult. The original auto route south from South Beach to Yachats required driving on the sand and avoiding high tides. Similarly, the dunes south of Florence remained remote.

Early outdoor recreators relied on stage travel to reach some destinations.

In addition to its beaches, the Siuslaw offered rivers full of salmonoid fishes. These were the Big and Little Nestucca, Salmon River, Siletz, Yaquina, Siuslaw, Alsea, Smith, and Umpqua. British sportsman and investor Wallis Nash visited Newport in 1877 and wrote about fly fishing in Marys River. [4]

> *The pool held another trout, though, who could not resist the sight of foreign flies; he turned out a nice plump fellow of about a quarter pound and lived under the roots of a tree at the lower end.*
>
> Wallis Nash *Oregon: There and Back in 1877*

After 1915, recreation cabin sites were available on most national forests in the West, including the Siuslaw. The recreation cabin program was generally successful, but for some reason, the Siuslaw's recreation cabin program did not flourish. In 1922 the Region 6 publication *Six Twenty-Six* reported that the Siuslaw had ten recreation cabin site permits in use. None remains today.

> **[The Siuslaw is] the only Forest in D-6 which has any sea beach, which when the Roosevelt Highway is completed will make it necessary to prepare a management plan for clam beds and crab fields...**
>
> ***Six Twenty-Six*, December 1926**

In addition to creating a special use permit system for private recreation cabins and commercial resorts and stores, the Term Occupancy Act of 1915 also made it possible for religious, fraternal, and other non-profit organizations to build camps and lodges on national forests. Four organizational camps built in the 1920s are associated with the Siuslaw. These are Meriwether, near Sand Lake on the Hebo Ranger District, a Mennonite Church camp on Drift Creek in the Hebo Ranger District, and Camp Baker and Camp Cleawox on the Oregon Dunes NRA. Meriwether and Baker are now privately owned by the sponsoring organization, which is the Boy Scouts. Cleawox, a Girl Scout camp, is located on a 45 acre special use permit tract. The camp remains in its original location on Cleawox Lake, but the lodge was rebuilt in 1995.

Recreation on the Siuslaw during the 1910s and 1920s—as on other national forests—relied on resorts and lodges, or cabins, to provide accommodations. There were private campgrounds and camping places on the Forest, but well-developed public

Automobile modified for rail travel, South Beach.

campgrounds were not yet available. The text to the 1934 map of the forest points out that lodging was mostly available at private facilities—"resorts which do not lie directly within the national forest, but are close to its boundary." Perhaps the most surprising part of 1910s and 1920s recreation on the Siuslaw is the difficulty of access. Travel by automobile or wagon and team along primitive roads was possible, but not convenient. The Forest Service map recommends railroads and even boats as a better alternative.

RECREATION

Recreation seekers find much to interest them in the western part of the Siuslaw National Forest and especially the region along the coast. When the interior valleys get too warm for comfort in the summer, this is the place to come. Spring is early, the climate is mild and pleasant along the seashore, and there is plenty to do. This region is an especially popular spring and early summer fishing ground and offers a great variety of fishing. Trout fishing with rod and fly in the smaller streams offers the best sport and good trout streams are plentiful. Fishing for silverside salmon with a casting rod and spoon, trolling for Chinook and other salmon, and deep sea fishing with the possibility of going after clams and crabs complete the list.

***Siuslaw National Forest Map*, 1934**

Cape Perpetua provided areas for picnics and camping.

RECREATION ON THE SIUSLAW AND ACCESS IN 1934		
RECREATION OPPORTUNITY	**ACTIVITIES AVAILABLE**	**GETTING THERE IN 1934**
Nestucca Bay, Devils Lake	Hunting & Fishing	Automobile via Willamina over the "new Salmon River road" (completed in 1930)
Drift Creek	Fishing	By boat from Taft, up the Siletz 8 miles, then 3 miles by foot trail
Table Mountain	Hunting	Auto or wagon from Alsea, then pack trail from Tidewater
Yachats	"First-class Camp"	Southern Pacific Railroad to Newport, then "half-days drive south from Newport"
Cape Perpetua	Camping, scenery	Not specified
Samaria (Mouth of Big Creek)	Private campgrounds	Not specified
Siuslaw Bay	Visiting Florence, Mapleton, Glenada	Southern Pacific Railroad from Eugene
Lakes Region	Hunting & Fishing	Southern Pacific Railroad from Eugene
Winchester Bay	Fishing	Railroad; "light draft boats" from the coast
Tenmile Lakes	Fishing	Southern Pacific Railroad from Eugene
Coos Bay	Hunting & Fishing	Southern Pacific Railroad from Eugene: "two-days travel from Allegany"; "large boats to North Bend or Marshfield"

Information from 1934 Siuslaw Recreation map.

AUTOMOBILE CAMPING ON THE SIUSLAW

During the 1930s, two events conspired to make automobile camping the primary recreation focus for the Siuslaw. The first of these was the completion of the Oregon Coast Highway with the necessary new bridges at Coos Bay, Reedsport, Florence, Waldport, and Newport. The auto route made access to the Siuslaw's coastal areas much more practical and convenient. The highway and the bridges were financed by the State of Oregon Department of Transportation and federal infrastructure programs including the Works Progress Administration (WPA).

Automobiles revolutionized forest camping.

The second event of the 1930s was the Civilian Conservation Corps and their dedication to building recreation facilities, including campgrounds, day-use areas, and scenic enhancements. Since the CCC was a national program of the New Deal, direction for CCC projects came from the top down. The Forest Service's nascent recreation program was a major beneficiary of CCC labor and the expertise of "local experienced men" hired to direct the CCC crews.

Did the CCC programs have a big influence on the Siuslaw?

Yes, they did. They built just about all the campgrounds on this Forest until oh, probably, about 1960. Anything prior to 1960—just about [all] as far as campgrounds were concerned—was built by the CCCs.

Ranger F. James Lyne Interview, 1987

CCC kitchen at Cape Perpetua, ca. 1936.

The new campgrounds featured designated camping spots, running water, restrooms, picnic tables, and stone fireplaces. Roads were stabilized with crushed rock to make them useable in the wet season. Some campgrounds built by the CCC had "community kitchens" that offered sheltered areas for cooking on rainy days. One remaining kitchen is located at the Hebo Lake campground. The CCC took many of the ideas for campground improvements and day-use amenities from Albert H. Good's influential book, *Park Structures and Facilities*.

The 1938 map of the Siuslaw shows the new campgrounds, the "Main Motor Highways," and "Secondary Routes." There were 14 campgrounds on the Forest in 1938. Presently, there are 44.

Improved Campgrounds, 1938

Alder Glen	**Rock Creek**
Rocky Bend	**Big Creek**
South Lake	**Sutton Lake**
Big Elk	**Siltcoos Outlet**
Maples	**Carter Lake**
Cape Perpetua	**Tahkenitch Lake**
Tenmile	**Eel Creek**

Most of the early automobile camping relied on tents, which were sometimes precarious on windy, rainy coastal nights. Early photos show that "travel trailers" and "teardrop trailers" were offering more stable accommodations than tents as early as the 1930s.

Early camp trailer.

CAMPGROUND LOCATIONS, 1938

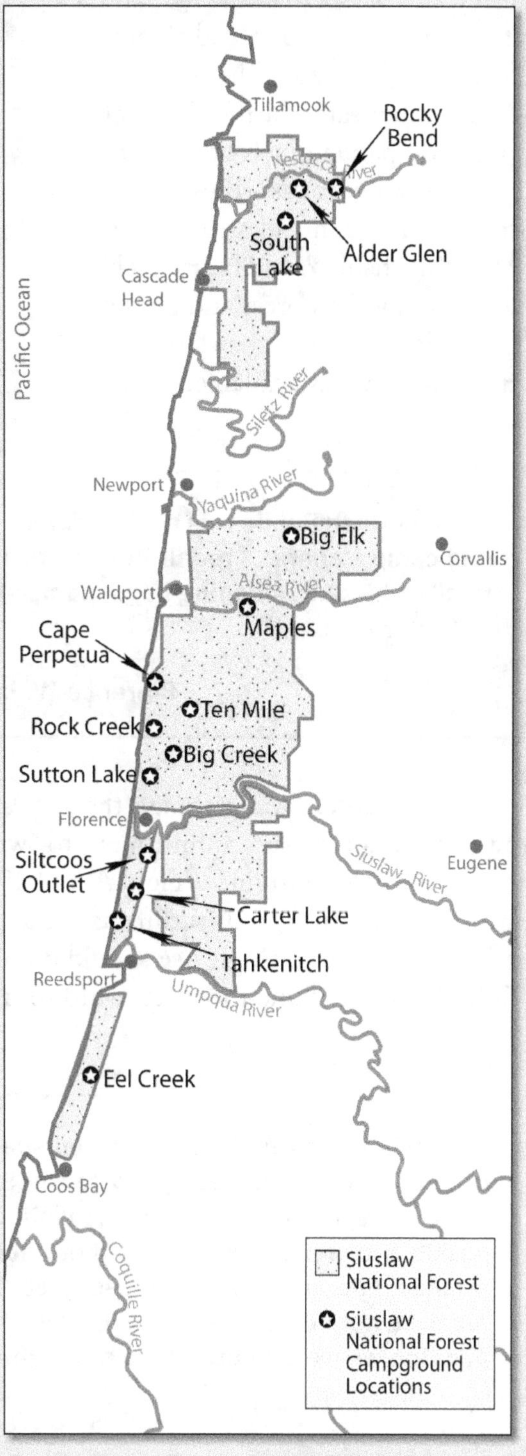

Tillamook
Rocky Bend
Nestucca River
South Lake
Alder Glen
Cascade Head
Pacific Ocean
Siletz River
Newport
Yaquina River
Big Elk
Corvallis
Waldport
Alsea River
Maples
Cape Perpetua
Ten Mile
Rock Creek
Big Creek
Sutton Lake
Florence
Siltcoos Outlet
Siuslaw River
Eugene
Carter Lake
Tahkenitch
Reedsport
Umpqua River
Eel Creek
Coos Bay
Coquille River
Siuslaw National Forest
Siuslaw National Forest Campground Locations

RECREATION PLANNING ON THE SIUSLAW IN THE 1950s AND 1960s

In the years after World War II, the demand for forest recreation grew. Leisure and prosperity enabled families to take longer vacations, and to buy recreation equipment. The increasing pace of timber sales during the 1950s and 1960s opened much of the Siuslaw with all-weather roads. These made formerly remote inland areas accessible for hunting, fishing, and berry-picking. Trails built by the Forest and by the CCC added hiking to the slate of recreation activities available.

Improvements at Tillicum Beach campground included pavement.

The American Public was getting "camping minded" and purchasing more pickups and camp trailers. I recall that it was in the summer of 1958 that I outfitted my family with tent, sleeping bags, camp stove, etc. and spent a wonderful weekend at Carter Lake.

Clarence W. Jacobs, *Working for the U.S. Forest Service*

As the nation moved through the 1950s, sentiment of the public and in Congress grew to favor a renewed commitment to "wise use" of the national forests. The result was the Multiple-Use Sustained-Yield Act of 1960. This legislation named timber, range, recreation, watershed, and wildlife as the appropriate uses of the national forests, with the provision that no single use should dominate to the exclusion of other uses. The term "Multiple-Use" became the watchword for inclusive planning.

The first money the Forest received specifically for recreation was in the summer of 1956, when I was assigned to the SO [Supervisor's Office] to do a recreation survey. I spent about six weeks visiting each district inventorying existing and possible campgrounds and other recreational sites. ...In 1958 Mike Clark, a landscape architect, was assigned to the SO. And then we on the districts received notice not to cut any old-growth trees along or near roads or streams. In addition we were not to make any clearcuts that were visible from certain roads.

Clarence W. Jacobs, *Working for the US Forest Service*

The first recreation plan [on the Siuslaw] started back in the CCC days. There was one that was written then. It was the first plan for the entire Forest. They had it in segments kind of before; they had it in different units. They had the Siltcoos Unit; then there was the Heceta Head/Perpetua Unit; there was the Hebo Unit. This was back in the CCC era when they first started writing those types of plans.

Ranger F. James Lyne Interview, 1980

Cover image, 1962 *Annual Report.*

In 1961 the Siuslaw recorded 944,400 recreational visits to the Forest.[5] The *Annual Report* titled "A Report on Multiple Use Management in 1962" featured a beach scene on the cover. Improvements for recreation in 1962 included increasing the capacity of parking lots at Siltcoos Beach Access, and completing campgrounds at Schooner Creek and Sutton Creek. New campgrounds offered pressure water and flush toilets. One of the chief concerns voiced in planning documents was controlling automobiles on the beaches and the dunes. The recreation program through the 1950s and 1960s could be seen as automobile-oriented.

During the turbulent 1960s, however, Congress passed two very important pieces of legislation that led recreation planning on the Siuslaw and other national forests away from the automobile-dominated strategies. These were the Wilderness Act of 1964 and the Wild and Scenic Rivers Act of 1968. In 1984, the Siuslaw created the Rock Creek, Drift Creek, and Cummins Creek Wilderness Areas. These are roadless areas on the Forest set aside for recreation without motor vehicles under the Oregon wilderness program.

Bicycling the coast highway has been popular since the 1930s.

One of the areas of the Siuslaw with special significance for recreation is Cape Perpetua. Acting Forest Superintendent J. Roy Harvey prepared an early planning memorandum on the Cape and "a small tract of land…at the mouth of Cape Creek."[6] Harvey noted that the Cape should not be opened to homestead entry under the 1906 Forest Homestead law because it was rugged and unsuitable for agriculture. He believed that the timber on the Cape Creek drainage would eventually be logged when a railroad was constructed along the coast.

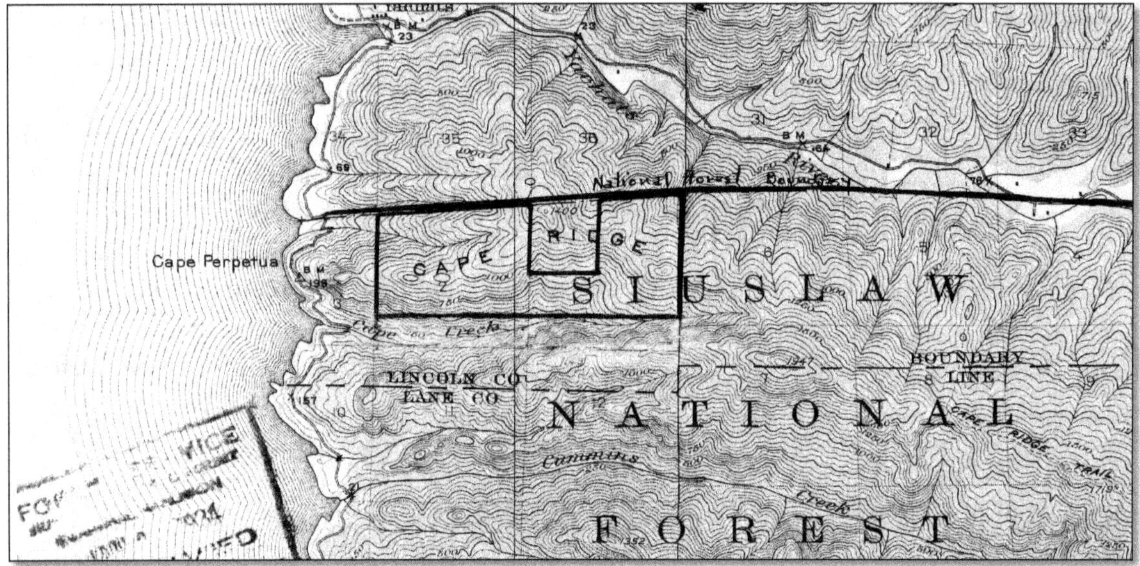

1934 map of Cape Perpetua Natural Area.

Harvey also realized the recreational potential that the Cape offered, and its unique proximity to the populous Willamette Valley.

> *The areas at the mouth of Cape Creek will also be of decided importance as a public campground as soon as the road around Cape Perpetua is completed. All similar lands or lands suitable for this purpose for many miles along the coast are alienated and it is now practically impossible for campers or tourists to secure suitable camping grounds without paying for the privilege.*
>
> *As soon as the road is completed along the coast it will be a very popular route for parties on short camping trips from the Willamette valley and adjacent towns, and there will undoubtedly be a very great demand for campgrounds.*
>
> Acting Forest Superintendent J. Roy Harvey, 1914

The railroad that Harvey envisioned was never built. Spruce Railroad XII, the Alsea Southern, came south from South Beach along the coast as far as the Blodgett Tract, but never reached Cape Perpetua. Even the road around the Cape was delayed through the 1920s. However, the Forest managed Cape Perpetua and the Cape Creek drainage as an area set aside from homestead entry and timber sales, although there was some salvage logging.

Cape Perpetua West Shelter is listed on the National Register of Historic Places.

In 1934, the Civilian Conservation Corps prepared a recreation plan for the "Perpetua-Heceta Recreational Unit."[7] This led to extensive recreational development at Cape Perpetua, including trails, vehicle access and parking, the stone parapets, and the spectacular stone trail shelter. In 1934, E.L. Kolbe proposed that the forest inland from the Cape be set aside as an official Forest Service Natural Area preserving the old-growth Sitka spruce-Western hemlock forest type. As Kolbe pointed out in his proposal, this type of forest was once common along the coasts of Oregon and Washington, but had been nearly eliminated by logging and fires in recent years. Preserving the Perpetua tract, Kolbe argued, would create what he called a "forest museum" for future study and enjoyment.

Kolbe proposed four recreational developments within or adjacent to the Cape Perpetua Natural Area. The first of these was the Perpetua Picnic Park and Camp, which was located on the Cape. In 1933 this park was under construction by the CCC as the crown jewel of their Perpetua-Heceta Recreational Unit. The second was a summer home site of ten acres on the Forest south of the Natural Area. This would be divided into individual lots and assigned to people wishing to build cabins under the Term Occupancy

Act program. The third recreational development would be an organizational site within the Natural Area. The fourth recreational development would be another summer home tract of six acres also within the Natural Area.

E.A. Sherman, Washington Office, and party view Cape Perpetua to the South, 1935.

The proposed Cape Perpetua Natural Area appeared on Forest maps after 1938. The organizational camp and summer home sites were never developed. During World War II, the military stationed lookouts and artillery on the Cape for three months.[8]

Starting in 1959, Richard Spray, Assistant Engineer on the Mapleton Ranger District, conducted a Forest-wide inventory of recreation resources under the National Forest Recreation Survey (NFRS). Cape Perpetua and the Dunes south of the Umpqua River qualified as scenic areas under Section U3 of the NFRS inventory scheme.[9] The Cape Perpetua Natural Area became the Cape Perpetua Scenic Area. Recreation Planner F. James Lyne prepared a recreation plan for the Forest in 1963 from the materials gathered in the NFRS inventory.[10] Lyne also prepared a separate management plan for the Cape in 1964. The Regional Forester approved the plan in 1967.

The new boundaries of the new scenic area extended west to the coast, north to the Forest boundary and included all of sections 2 and 3 and the northern portion of sections 10 and 11 south to the Lincoln/Lane county line.

Campgrounds built by the CCC offered rustic amenities.

By 1974 developments at the Cape included the Devils Churn viewpoint, the Cape Perpetua viewpoint, the Cape Perpetua campground, the new Visitor Center, and 4.9 miles of hiking trails. Future developments expanded the acreage of the scenic areas, added miles of hiking trails, and put in an underpass to create a safe highway crossing.

Cape Perpetua remains one of the most spectacular scenic areas on the Oregon coast. As of 2008, the Forest Service has provided formal planning and protection for the Cape for 94 years.

Cape Perpetua Visitor Center was dedicated in 1967.

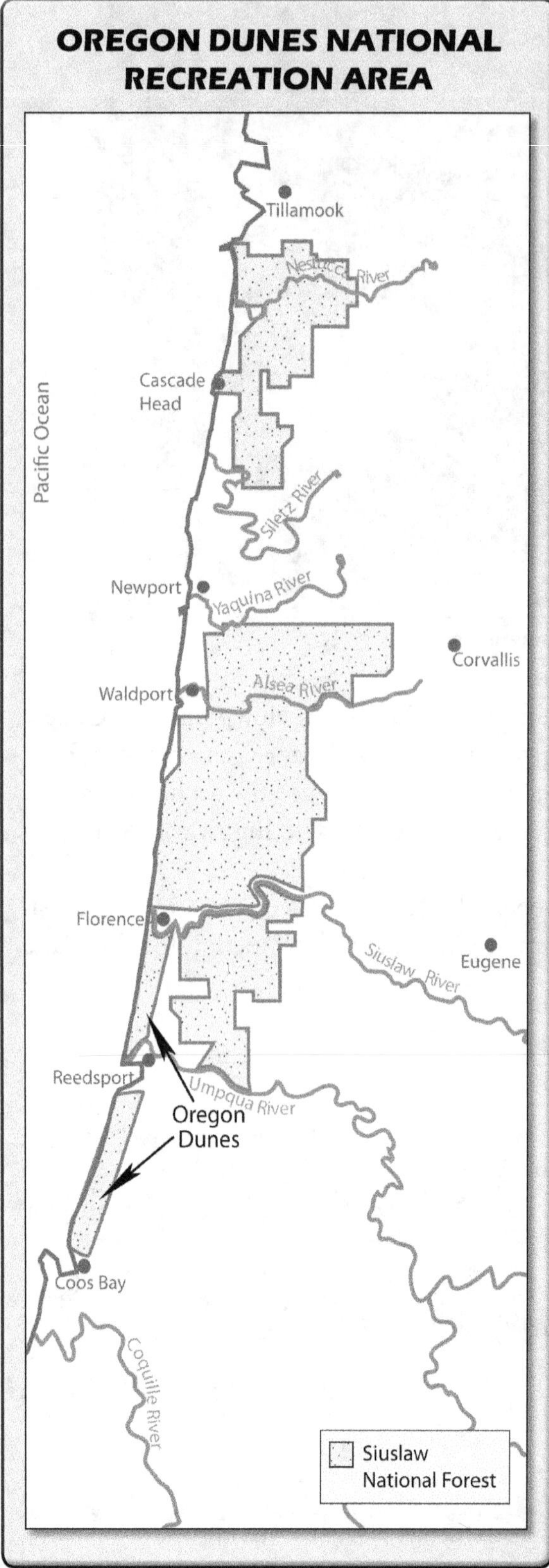

The Oregon Dunes consist of beachfront parcels of the Forest extending south from Florence to Coos Bay for a combined length of 46 miles of coastline. Prior to the formation of the Umpqua Forest Reserve, Euro-American settlers had filed on lands within the Dunes, but their efforts at homesteading were not successful. In the northern part of the Dunes, for example, 2,300 acres had been claimed but only two or three settlers remained on their claims by 1919.[11]

Early settlers and Forest Service managers tried to contain the shifting sand to keep it from engulfing patented lands, roads, and even lakes. The most common strategy involved planting European beachgrass, Scotch broom, and shore pine. These plants prospered on the Dunes, but the beachgrass and Scotch broom became nuisance species that were nearly uncontrollable. The European beachgrass reduced the areas where the endangered snowy plover could successfully nest.

During the first decades of the twentieth century, Forest managers and Oregonians in general did not see the Dunes offering a great recreation potential. With the exception of a few homesteaders trying to cultivate cranberry bogs, people avoided the area through the 1920s and 1930s. While the Dunes themselves were not popular, the large lakes immediately east of the Dunes attracted the recreating public. Camping and fishing at Woahink, Siltcoos, Tahkenitch, Eel, and Tenmile lakes—all east of the Forest but adjacent

The only areas [on the Forest] which have no cover are the sand dunes along the coast. These sand dunes occupy a comparatively narrow strip of land extending along the beach. They have no agricultural value. They are largely barren, but in many places scrubby shore pine, spruce, and fir have found a foothold and established a windbreak, which protects adjacent farm and forest lands from the shifting sands. These areas have little value for the production of timber, but they should be permanently retained as part of the National Forest for experimental and investigative purposes, and the protection they will afford surrounding land when they are fully reclaimed.

Siuslaw National Forest Land Classification Inventory, 1919

to the Dunes—were popular destinations. The 1934 Siuslaw National Forest map publicized the "Lakes Region" of the Forest as Siltcoos, Woahink, Tahkenitch, and Tenmile, all a mile or two east of the Forest. There were commercial tourist accommodations on the lakes, and each was served by the Southern Pacific Railroad branch line from Eugene.

Siltcoos Lake bass, 1958.

Only Cleawox Lake was located within the Forest boundaries, and it was not readily accessible by rail. As automobile roads improved during the 1930s, Forest managers began to take notice of Cleawox. In 1937 Edmund Meola, Landscape Architect, presented plans for "The Design and Construction of the Cleawox Lake Organization Tract" to the Forest Supervisor. Meola's initial plans were well-

Water sports on the lakes near the Oregon Dunes.

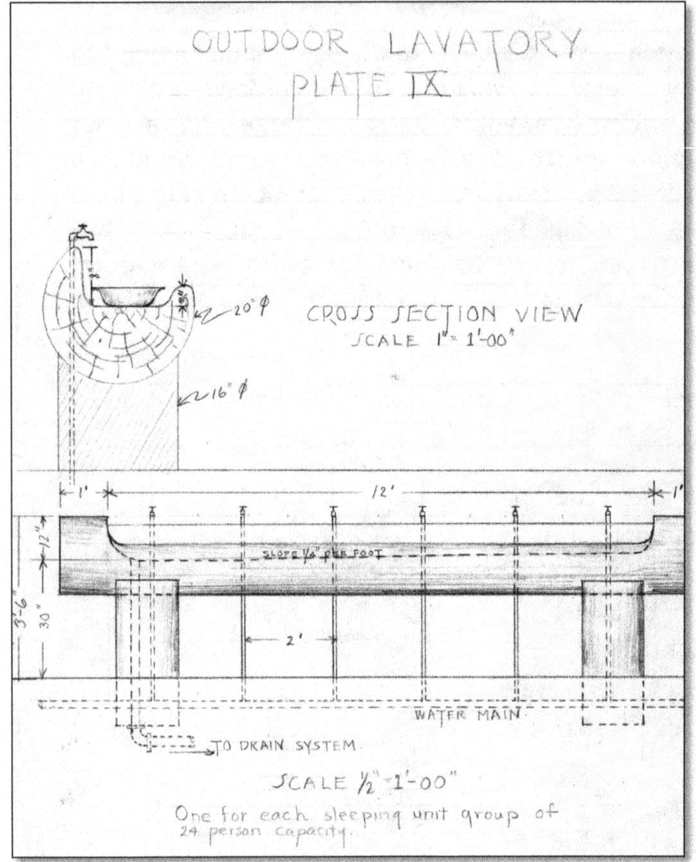

Plans for Cleawox Camp included rustic details such as this lavatory, 1937.

conceived, but Ralph Shelley, Forest Supervisor, felt that they lacked sufficient "specific detail and requirements" and he would not approve them.[12] However, the Cleawox Organizational Camp was built a few years later, and occupied by the Girl Scouts under special use permit. The original lodge was recognized as an outstanding example of Rustic architecture.

Civilian Conservation Corps recreational development on the Dunes consisted of four campgrounds. These were Siltcoos Outlet and Carter Lake near Siltcoos Lake, Tahkenitch campground, and Eel Creek campground near Eel Lake.

After World War II, with the spread of motor vehicle recreation, the Dunes themselves became popular with "dune buggy" enthusiasts who drove their home-made vehicles through the sandy landscape. In 1959 Oregon Senator Richard Neuberger introduced legislation to make the Dunes a National Seashore and bring it under the administration of the National Park Service, a branch of the Department of the Interior.

Home-made dune buggies predominated before the 1970s.

Forest Service managers opposed Neuberger's plan because they did not want to relinquish control of what was becoming an important recreation draw for the

Siuslaw. At the same time, the Forest Service and the National Park Service were in conflict over the proposed North Cascades National Park in Washington.[13] Acrimony between the USDA Forest Service and the Department of the Interior dates back to the conflict between Richard Ballinger and Gifford Pinchot in 1909. The compromise between the two federal agencies was that the North Cascades became a National Park under the Department of the Interior, and the Oregon Dunes became a National Recreation Area and remained part of the Siuslaw National Forest.

> ***How did the local officials on the Siuslaw feel at that time? Were they pushing for one resolution or another on the Oregon Dunes?***
>
> **They were...but they could not come out publicly and say so....But what went on behind the scenes, you talked to some of the local people that were opposed to the Park Service coming in, and so you let them do the talking for you.**
>
> **Ranger F. James Lyne Interview, 1980**

Legislation passed in Congress on March 23, 1972, established the Oregon Dunes National Recreation Area. The Final Environmental Impact Statement and the Oregon Dunes NRA Management Plan was published July 12, 1994. Management directions for the new NRA sought a "mix of recreational settings and opportunities" that would encompass highly developed campgrounds as well as natural areas and opportunities for "non-motorized recreation experiences in undeveloped areas." However, the Plan acknowledged that the Dunes were "widely recognized within the ORV [Off-Road Vehicle] community as one of the premier riding areas in the country." Much of the Plan was devoted to regulation of ORVs in what was recognized as a fragile and unique landscape.

Management of the Dunes required restricting vehicle access to fragile environments.

At the northern end of the Siuslaw, the Sand Lake dunes on the Hebo Ranger District offered a landscape and recreational potential similar to the Oregon Dunes. The area is located immediately south of Cape Lookout, and twelve miles south of Tillamook. Camp Meriweather, a Boy Scout Camp, is located there. By the end of the 1970s,

The Sand Lake dunes provide many recreational opportunities.

off-road vehicle enthusiasts had discovered the Sand Lake dunes. Although the use was much less than on the Oregon Dunes, conflicts between ORV riders, the public, and land managers led to the formulation of a long-term plan in 1980.

The Sand Lake Planning Area, as defined by the plan, included 1,076 acres of the Siuslaw, 314 acres of Tillamook County land, 41 acres of Oregon State Parks land, and 500 acres of Oregon Division of State Lands land. The plan addressed issues of sanitation, traffic and use, administration, and law enforcement. Also, as the Snowy Plover nesting habitat was raising concerns by the late 1970s, environmental protection was another significant area of concern and compromise.[14]

Like the Oregon Dunes NRA, Sand Lake offers an example of the continuity of Forest Service stewardship. Scenic resources like Cape Perpetua were easily recognizable as compelling attractions, but Sand Lake and the Dunes NRA required some time and imagination to find their places among the Siuslaw's best recreational resources.

NOTES

1 Gifford Pinchot, *The Use of the National Forests* (Washington, DC: USGPO, 1907) 13.

2 See William C. Tweed "Recreation Site Planning and Improvement in National Forests 1891-1942," (Washington, DC: USDA Forest Service History Section, 1980) 4.

3 "Vacation Suggestions, Yaquina Bay, 1898" quoted in Richard Price, *Newport Oregon: 1866-1936, Portrait of a Coastal Resort* (Newport, OR: LCHS, 1975) 38.

4 Wallis Nash, *Oregon: There and Back in 1877* (Corvallis, OR: Oregon State University Press, 1976) 136.

5 Siuslaw Annual Report, 1962, 8.

6 J. Roy Harvey, Memorandum of July 31, 1914, Settlement Files, #339 (on file, Waldport, OR: Siuslaw NF, 1914).

7 This plan was approved by the Siuslaw National Forest March 12, 1932.

8 Cape Perpetua Scenic Area Plan, 1974, 4; Richard Spray Interview, 2008.

9 Richard Spray Interview.

10 F. James Lyne Interview (Corvallis, OR: Heritage Associates, 1998) 91.

11 Stephen D. Beckham, Kathryne Toepel, and Rick Minor, *Cultural Resource Overview of the Siuslaw National Forest* (Corvallis, OR: Siuslaw NF, 1982) 245-246.

12 Meola's plans and Shelley's comments are on file, Siuslaw National Forest.

13 F. James Lyne Interview, 132.

14 USDA Forest Service, Environmental Assessment, Sand Lake Management Plan, 1980, 9.

CHAPTER EIGHT

FINISHING THE CENTURY

The last decades of the Siuslaw's century saw the Forest moving away from its post-war focus on timber production, and responding to national and regional legislative mandates. Beginning with the Multiple Use Sustained Yield Act of 1960, Congress restated a fundamental management philosophy for the Forest Service by placing watershed, range, wildlife, and recreation as equal priorities with timber.

In the years since World War II, timber had been increasingly important for most national forests, including the Siuslaw. By the late 1950s, however, national forest timber production was becoming controversial. Conservation groups—most notably the Sierra Club—led opposition to Forest Service management practices. The public and local newspaper editors responded to several general conservation issues, especially clear-cutting and wildlife.

On the positive side, high timber production on the national forests provided logs to keep the mills running when private timber supply was depleted from World War II demand and the liquidation that occurred during the depression. The heavy annual cuts of the post-war years produced revenue for the Forest Service that made the agency less dependent on Congressional appropriations. Revenue-sharing programs meant that local communities received as much as 25 percent of timber revenue in lieu of property tax. In addition, the network of new logging roads opened the forest to the public and helped forest managers deal with fire and silvicultural activities.

Alsea District watershed damage, clear-cut slope on left.

The negative aspects of intense timber production included the damage that logging did to watersheds, especially on steep slopes. For the Siuslaw and other Douglas fir forests, intensive logging was accomplished through clear-cutting, which was always controversial. Spawning and rearing areas for anadronomous fishes were damaged in streams adjacent to heavy cutting. The loss of old-growth habitat threatened certain species of wildlife.

After the passage of the Multiple Use Sustained Yield Act, proposed by Senator Hubert Humphrey in 1960, the Forest was required to publish annual plans for multiple resource use. In the 1962 Siuslaw National Forest "Report on Multiple Use Management," Forest Supervisor Spencer T. Moore prefaced the document with a quotation from Gifford Pinchot: "We have to the best of

National Environmental Legislation 1960-1976

- **Multiple Use Sustained Yield Act, 1960**
- **Accelerated Public Works Program (Job Corps), 1963-1964**
- **Wilderness Act, 1964**
- **Wild and Scenic Rivers Act, 1968**
- **National Environmental Policy Act, 1969**
- **Endangered Species Act, 1973**
- **National Forest Management Act, 1976**

I got to write the original management plan for the three wilderness areas here on the Waldport district: Drift Creek, Cummins Creek and Rock Creek. I was able to, from past experience, write in those plans some restrictions which I think is very significant. First, I decided to have one wilderness completely trailless. It had no trails at that point. It was important for a total watershed involvement to have no trails there. The other was, we had some established grazing in Drift Creek, but it had been terminated ten years prior. Over the years, I had developed more trails into the Drift Creek country. I felt that should not be done, since we had no established use, or existing use. I wrote those up so that they would be horseless wildernesses. Pack stock and stuff is a very important issue in some of the eastside wilderness [areas]. Westside, where the soils were always damp and stuff, a resource problem could very quickly get started. I wrote those up to be horseless. I'm here working on this pretty independently, and the Ranger just said "do it". I wrote that in there. He questioned that. He signed it and sent it on. It went to the Supervisors office in Corvallis, and it went on to the regional office in Portland, where it got reviewed up there. They applauded that decision as being visionary. It was the first it had ever happened in this region, to have a horseless wilderness. So then everyone kind of breathed a sigh of relief and, of course, they were quite willing to accept the responsibility for that.

Loyd Collett Interview, 2005

our ability managed your lands within our jurisdiction to provide 'the greatest good for the greatest number in the long run.'"[1] This was well-chosen, for it made the point that multiple use was not new and that the Chief Forester himself had set the Forest Service on this path in 1905.

Recreation was the most familiar of the new multiple use objectives. This was a use that had been important since the 1930s and was more important in the post-war years. The legislation of the 1960s put a new slant on recreation by opening the discussion of wilderness areas and wild and scenic rivers. The Siuslaw eventually designated three wilderness areas under the Oregon Wilderness Act of 1984: Drift Creek, Cummins Creek, and Rock Creek. Although the Forest has an abundance of rivers, none was designated as Wild and Scenic.

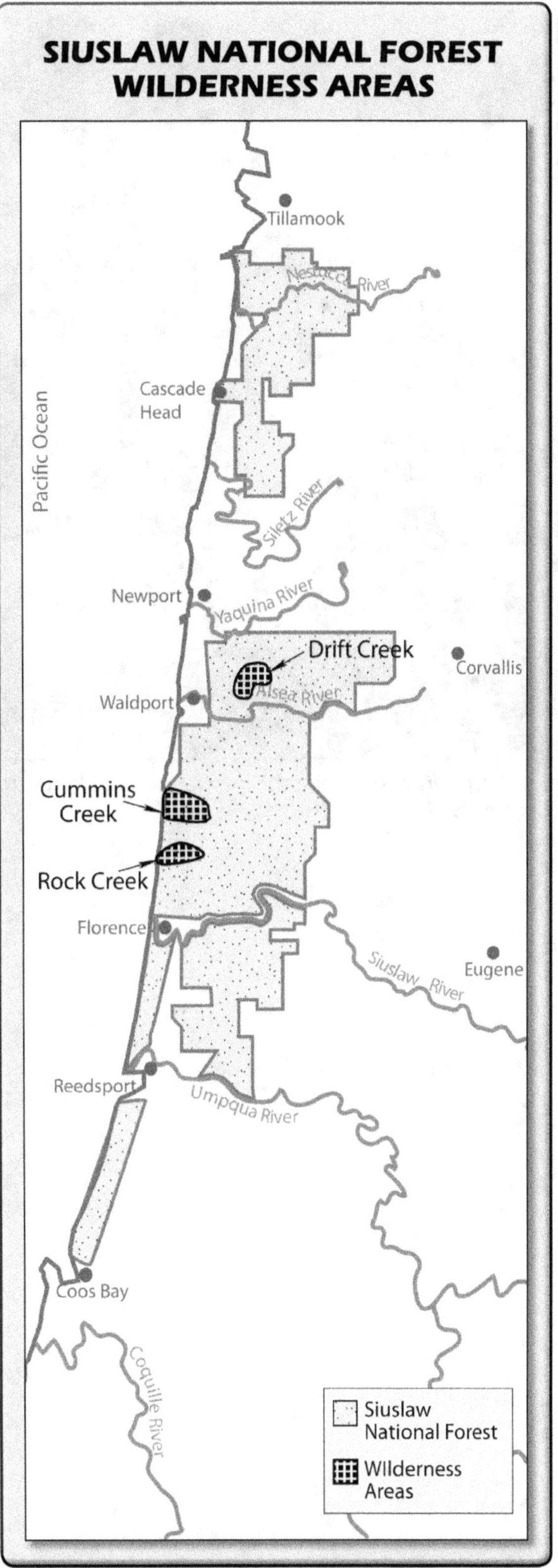

Another 1960s legislative thrust, the Accelerated Public Works Program of 1963, created opportunities for young people to enter programs run by the Department of Labor, including the Youth Conservation Corps and the Job Corps. These were similar in some ways to the Civilian Conservation Corps of the 1930s, but not solely dedicated to conservation. The Job Corps—which was a part of this program—was not as large as the CCC, but it was considerably longer lived. The program began in 1964 and is still operating.

The Department of Labor and the Forest Service chose Camp Angell as a Job Corps center. It is one of six Job

Job Corps enrollees paint the interior of Cape Perpetua Visitor Center, 1967.

Corps programs in Oregon. This early co-ed facility incorporated some of the original structure built by the CCC in 1941. When the Job Corps came to Camp Angell in the 1960s, they found an aging camp in need of updating. The program has found sufficient support from the public and from Congress to continue. Projects included the Cape Perpetua Visitors' Center, the Alsea Ranger Station, the Hebo Ranger District office, and expanding the Waldport Ranger Station.

NATIONAL ENVIRONMENTAL POLICY ACT AND THE "OLOGISTS"

Of all the legislation of the 1960s and 1970s, the National Environmental Policy Act or NEPA has had the most impact on Forest Service policy and practices. This Act was introduced by Senator Henry M. Jackson and Congressman John Dingle in 1969, and signed into law in 1970. The NEPA requires an environmental analysis for all major projects, including timber sales. The NEPA also calls for public involvement and comment in the decision-making process. As a result of these requirements, the Forest Service hired many specialists in scientific fields during the 1970s, including biologists, hydrologists, geologists, archaeologists, and others collectively called "ologists" by old-time Forest Service staff. Although the Forest Service had long employed specialists for research and specific projects, the new scientific staff members were working on the ranger districts and in forest supervisors' offices.

Karen Bennett, hydrologist, 1989.

Another environmental law created during the 1970s was the Endangered Species Act of 1973. This legislation would have a huge effect on the Siuslaw and other national forests in the 1990s.

So we needed a wildlife biologist, and we needed a soil scientist and a hydrologist. Well, those people are called the "'ologists" in the Forest Service. They weren't as much interested in fighting fire. You know, they got their degree, they went to college to be a soil scientist or a fish biologist, and they had no interest in fighting fire. So as we started hiring those folks, ...[our] workforce now is specialized and they all had an interest in their specialty and not in other realms of the Forest Service, which fire was the big one in the summer. Not saying we don't have biologists and soil people that go out and fight fires now, but a lot of them don't. They're more concentrated on their careers, missions, being a biologist.

Dave Beck Interview, 2004

Important changes within the culture of the Forest Service occurred during this period. Forest Service hiring and recruiting changed to create a more diverse workforce, and to include the new specialties needed for NEPA planning. As a result, the Forest Service could no longer rely exclusively on workers from local communities and forestry programs at land-grant colleges.

Women weren't allowed to wear pants to work. It started when some of the teachers, especially kindergarten teachers, were insisting on wearing slacks to work because they had to be down on the floor with the kids and dresses just weren't working. Then the other government workers thought we ought to be able to wear our [jeans], and I was on the Umpqua then. The AO said that women absolutely would not be wearing dresses while he was here or pants suits or anything else while he was in charge. And he retired. I was a forestry tech by then and wore jeans a lot, in and out of the office, so the other women in the office said to the ranger, "If Pauline can wear pants to work why can't we?" He couldn't see any reason why not. Actually, I think he was afraid to tackle that one, and so we wore nice slacks to work and looked very attractive and then Glide was the first district that did that.

Pauline McGinty Interview, 2006

Women made up a larger portion of the Forest Service staff after the 1980s.

The new personnel were not always as comfortable with the agency or with living and working in small isolated communities as their predecessors had been. Also, some of the new staff were not entirely convinced of the Forest Service's good faith in environmental stewardship. Concerned Forest Service employees in Eugene formed the Forest Service Employees for Environmental Ethics (FSEEE) during this period. In its own words, the FSEEE serves as "a vigilant watchdog over the successes and failures of the Forest Service. Our efforts to reform the agency require FSEEE to widely publicize examples such as disastrous timber policies and successful watershed restorations."[2]

I don't think we as an organization or agency are as connected to the local community as we used to be. And having come from that community, I think I can make that statement fairly without being overly critical of both the outfit I work for and the community I come from. Employees here are still... pretty involved in the local community. But the Forest Service back when I came to work here, and I know before that because I know a lot of those old-timers and for a number of years after I came to work here, was viewed as a primary contributor. People here were very visible and involved in local service clubs, volunteer organizations. We were actively a part of the Chamber of Commerce. We participated in the Community Days event. We don't do that very much anymore.

Bruce Gainer Interview, 2005

The 1970s were a time of cultural change in many aspects of American life. Leisure activities became more important, manufacturing industries declined, and ordinary people became concerned—and opinionated—about the environment. Such disparate phenomena as the media, the Vietnam War, and the drug culture influenced people's outlook. On the Siuslaw, pressure increased as more people from the Willamette Valley and metropolitan areas came to the Forest for recreation. The creation of the Oregon Dunes National Recreation Area in 1972 shows the agency's increasing interest in recreation and the larger place it was assuming in forest management.

During these years, the Forest Service became concerned about law enforcement and the need to protect visitors and staff. Threats included misuse of resources by visitors, eco-terrorism, and marijuana cultivation. Retired Siuslaw Law Enforcement Officer (LEO) Bruce Gainer commented in an interview that there were 23 LEOs in Region 6 at the start of the 1970s, and over 120 by the 1980s. Gainer himself logged over 1500 hours in a helicopter searching for marijuana plantations on the Siuslaw. At the peak of activity, Gainer found over 200 plots in one year.[3] Eco-terrorism began in the 1970s and continued through the 1980s and 1990s. On the Siuslaw, protestors burned herbicide helicopters in 1980. The destruction of the Oakridge Ranger Station on the nearby Willamette National Forest in 1996 was one of the most visible terrorist actions.

The forest issue that defined the 1970s and 1980s was clear-cutting. Silviculturalists advocated clear-cutting as the most efficient and cost-effective strategy for logging and replanting Douglas fir forests. Evidence from studies at the University of Washington and other institutions supported the practice.[4] Critics of the practice brought up its negative effects on the landscape and on wildlife. Finally, two national forests far from the Douglas fir country—the Bitterroot National Forest in western Montana and the Monongahela National Forest in West Virginia—were the setting for serious confrontations between environmental groups and the Forest Service. Environmental groups sued, and the courts ruled against the Forest Service. In 1976, Congress passed legislation to regulate clear-cutting on Oregon and California lands administered by the Forest Service and the Bureau of Land Management. These laws mandated additional environmental planning, required management for species diversity, and limited clear-cutting to 40 or 60 acre plots.

Stream washout, 1990.

On the Siuslaw, two environmental lawsuits had important consequences for forest management. These were the Gilmore suit in 1972 and the Mapleton suit in 1984. The Gilmore suit came as the environmental community's response to serious landslides on steep clear-cut slopes. Slides on the Bell Divide sale ran into Fivemile Creek, a tributary of Tahkenitch Lake. The outcome of the Gilmore suit was that the courts suspended logging in the south end of the Gardiner Ranger District. The Mapleton suit suspended logging on sales on the Mapleton District requiring road construction. Sales were permitted on a case-by-case basis for several years until the judgment was overturned.[5]

Log truck protest, 1976.

INTO THE 1990s

Through the 1970s and 1980s, the Siuslaw and other forests in Region 6 incorporated the new planning procedures and management objectives into their operations. Timber sales continued at a substantial pace on the Siuslaw, with yearly volumes ranging from a low of 254.8 million board feet sold in Fiscal Year (FY) 1989 to a high of 406.6 million board feet sold in FY 1981. Yearly sales from FY 1980 to FY 1990 averaged 344 million board feet. The cut consisted of second-growth Douglas fir, western hemlock, and some Sitka spruce, mostly trees in the 100-150 year age range. These trees were natural reproduction after the huge forest fires of the mid-1800s. Herbicide applications and clear-cuts drew protests during the 1980s, and both of these practices received attention from the media, especially in the urban areas of Portland and Eugene. Herbicide applications in the Alsea Valley prompted a large protest on the Forest.

Events of the 1990s

- **Siuslaw National Forest *Land and Resource Management Plan*, 1990**
- **Northern Spotted Owl listed as endangered, 1990**
- **Marbled Murrelet listed as endangered, 1992**
- **Snowy Plover listed as endangered, 1993**
- **Clinton Environmental Summit, Portland, April, 1993**
- ***Forest Ecosystem Management*, July, 1993**
- **Draft Supplemental EIS for Spotted Owl zone, July, 1993**
- **Final Supplemental EIS for Spotted Owl zone, February, 1994**
- ***Record of Decision for Amendments to Forest Service and Bureau of Land Management Planning Documents within the Range of the Northern Spotted Owl* (aka The *Northwest Forest Plan*), April, 1994**
- **Siuslaw National Forest *Forest Plan Merger Document*, December 1996**

In 1990, the Siuslaw prepared its *Land and Resource Management Plan*. Other national forests in Region 6 prepared comprehensive plans in the same year. These were substantial documents prepared in accordance with the National Environmental Policy Act of 1969 and the National Forest Management Act of 1976. The Siuslaw's 1990 plan was to remain in force through a 10-year cycle, with revisions scheduled in 2000. The plan was to establish the following:

- Forest-wide multiple-use goals
- Forest wide strategy to meet NFMA requirements
- Management areas within the Forest and their specific requirements

- Allowable timber volumes
- Evaluation and monitoring strategy[6]

The major issues listed in the 1990 plan consisted of 25 items, all of which were at least somewhat contentious. The top six were timber, old-growth forest, watershed, fish habitat, wildlife and endangered species, and recreation. The northern spotted owl had recently been listed as an endangered species, so the *Plan* designated 13,587 acres of old-growth forest as spotted owl habitat that would not be logged. The total old-growth reserve was 30,807 acres in the 1990-2000 decade and 23,329 acres in subsequent decades.[7] Timber volume for the 1990-2000 decade was to average 332 million board feet each year.

Marbled murrelet.

We found the first [marbled murrelet] nest in Oregon in 1990. There were no nests known in Oregon to my knowledge until 1988, and there was only one nest known in North America and that was found in 1977 down in the Olympic State Park and that was found accidentally. So actually the Audubon Society has put out a reward for the first person to find a marbled murrelet nest because it was the last species in North America that hadn't been found. And that nest was found accidentally in 1977. So up until the early part, I think, the late 80s and early 90s that research really began on the murrelet.

Kim Nelson Interview, 2004

I think it was about 1990 that the marbled murrelet/spotted owl issue came on board, and we kind of were in a transition mode for a time. There was a time when we got away from planning and did things like marbled murrelet surveys. Doing recreation work, which was something different for me, but we couldn't do the planning like we used to. It had to be other things. We had to transition to other things.

Bruce Buckley Interview, 2004

The northern spotted owl was listed as endangered in 1990. Listings for the marbled murrelet, coho salmon, the snowy plover, and other species found on the Siuslaw followed. The region-wide 1990 planning effort came under criticism in the courts, and the courts ordered the forests within the northern spotted owl's range to suspend timber production and other management activities until issues could be resolved. In 1993, President Clinton called for an environmental conference to be held in Portland in April. The conference would examine the controversy and propose solutions. President Clinton mandated an inter-agency group called the Forest Ecosystem Management Assessment Team (FEMAT). In July of 1993, FEMAT published its report, called *Forest Ecosystem Management: an Ecological, Economic, and Social Assessment.*

President Clinton's Environmental Summit, Portland, 1993.

In the wake of the FEMAT report, the Forest Service and the Bureau of Land Management created an interagency team to prepare an Environmental Impact Statement (designated the "Supplemental Environmental Impact Statement" or SEIS) to

Timber cutting and other operations on lands managed by the Forest Service and the Bureau of Land Management within the range of the northern spotted owl have been brought virtually to a halt by federal court orders for several reasons. Foremost has been the failure of the agencies to produce plans that satisfy the requirements of several laws including the National Forest Management Act of 1976, the Endangered Species Act of 1979, and the National Environmental Policy Act of 1969. Shortcomings have included delays in meeting court-imposed time schedules, inadequate environmental impact statements, and numerous proposed management actions (e.g. timber sale proposals) that resulted in "jeopardy opinions" from the U.S. Department of the Interior, Fish and Wildlife Service.

***Forest Ecosystem Management: an Ecological, Economic, and Social Assessment* [the FEMAT Report]**

Agencies contributing to the FEMAT Report

- **US Department of Agriculture, Forest Service**
- **US Department of Commerce, National Marine Fisheries Service**
- **US Department of the Interior, Bureau of Land Management**
- **US Department of the Interior, Fish and Wildlife Service**
- **US Department of the Interior, National Park Service**
- **Environmental Protection Agency**

serve as a planning document for the national forests and BLM's O&C lands within the range of the northern spotted owl. This area included forests and O&C lands throughout western Washington, western Oregon, and northern California. The 1990 Siuslaw Forest Plan and Forest Plans for eight other forests in Region 6 would be affected by the new supplemental EIS. The supplemental EIS was available in draft in July, 1993, and in its final form in February, 1994. Two months later, the interagency group published the "Record of Decision" for amending previous plans of national forests and O&C lands within the range of the northern spotted owl. This document is generally known as the *Northwest Forest Plan*.

Fairly early on, we recognized that this critter [the northern spotted owl] was going to be fairly difficult to manage just because they use such large areas and they seem to like old forests. Of course, back in those days (this was the early '70s through about the early '80s) the management agencies were not really prepared to deal with something like that. The focus was mainly on producing wood volume. That's where most of our direction was coming from. So fairly early on we recognized that there was somewhat of a conflict there.

Eric Forsman, member of the FEMAT team, Interview, 2004

The *Northwest Forest Plan* follows Alternative 9 of the FEMAT report. The *Plan* established that the range of the northern spotted owl on federal land consisted of more than 24 million acres. This land was to be managed as follows:

Congressionally Reserved Lands—30% of the range, consisting of National Parks, Wildlife Refuges, Wilderness Areas, and Wild and Scenic River corridors, was already protected by previous legislation.

Late Successional Reserves—30% of the range, consisting of forests to be managed as old growth or mature coniferous forests could not be logged.

Adaptive Management Areas—6% of the range, consisting of lands open to experimental management strategies, could be logged on a trial basis.

Managed Late Successional Areas—1% of the range, consisting of late successional forest land not necessarily managed as reserves, could be logged.

Administrative Withdrawals—6% of the range, designated as administrative sites by the Forest Service, was already protected.

Riparian Reserves—11% of the range, consisting of lands reserved for watershed management, could not be logged.

Matrix—The remaining 16% of the northern spotted owl's range was available for logging.

In effect, 78 percent of the national forest and O&C land within the northern spotted owl range was reserved and was not available for timber harvest. Twenty-two percent—the matrix lands and the "adaptive management areas"—would be available for timber sales. Authors of the *Plan* estimated that timber volume from all federal lands within the range of the northern spotted owl would dwindle to 1.1 billion board feet.[8] This would be the total cut for all national forests and O&C lands within the northern spotted owl habitat. For comparison, the Siuslaw alone cut 420 million board feet, or about 38% of this amount in 1988.

The Siuslaw set about incorporating directions from the *Northwest Forest Plan* into an amended version of its 1990 *Lands and Resource Management Plan.* The resulting "Forest Plan Merger Document" was published in December of 1996. The effects on the Siuslaw were profound. Timber sales diminished from 381.7 million board feet in 1990 to 12.4 million in 1991, and then to 4.2 million in 1992. Other activities, however, would flourish in the new environment. These included stream restoration projects, heritage projects, and wildlife management.

In summary, I would generalize by saying that the Forest Service has been accused of practicing industrial forestry on public lands and found guilty, although we did it as well or better than anyone. But there is no right way to do the wrong thing. Now we need to develop a new art, that of ecosystem management.

Forest Supervisor James Furnish, 1994

The Siuslaw is not the only source of timber for the coast, of course, and the highly productive state forests and private lands have contributed most of the total cut for western Washington and Oregon. Private forests and state forests are not governed by the *Northwest Forest Plan*, but they are required to develop Habitat Conservation Plans on 100-year planning cycles.

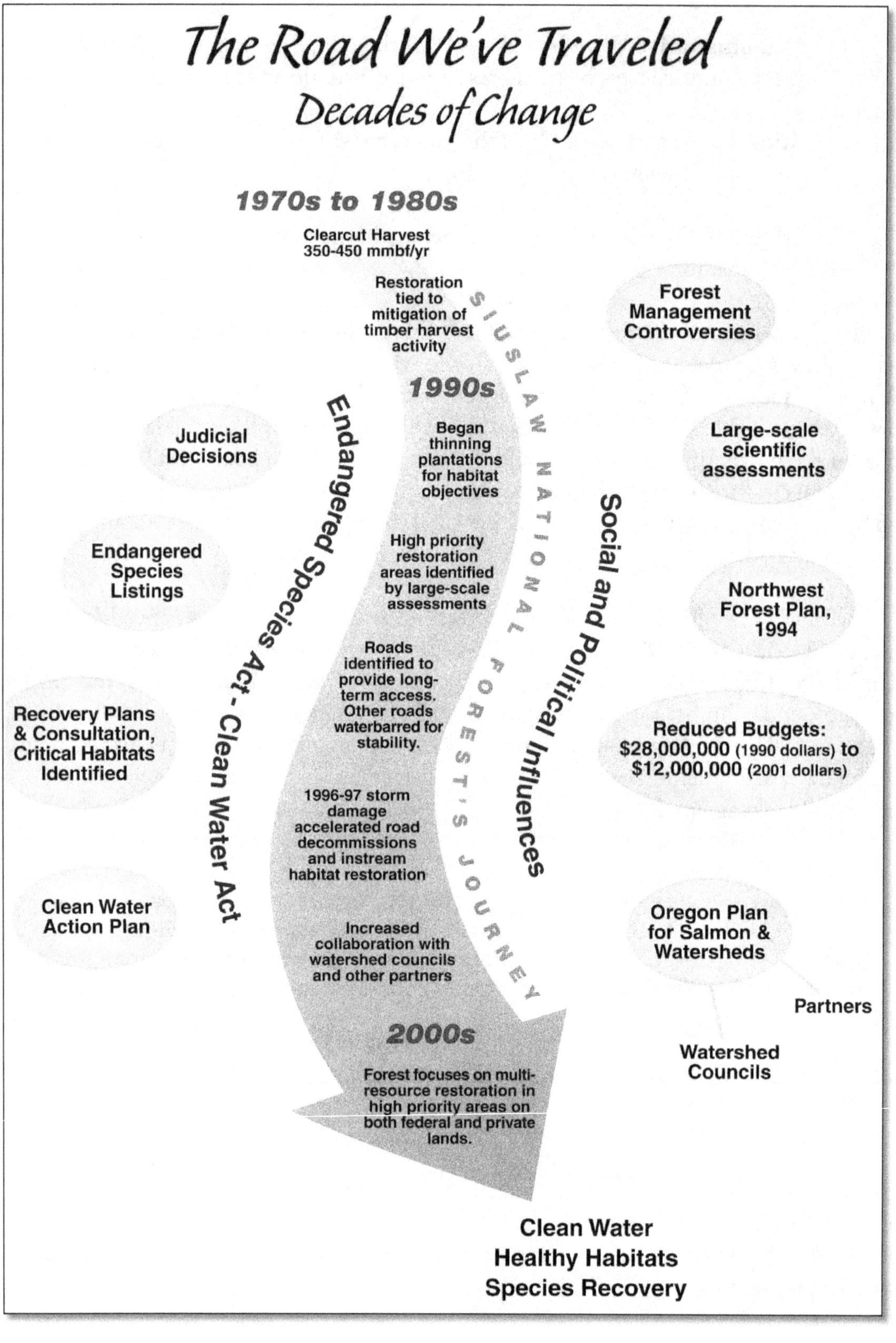

The Road We've Traveled

Decades of Change

1970s to 1980s

Clearcut Harvest
350-450 mmbf/yr

Restoration tied to mitigation of timber harvest activity

SIUSLAW NATIONAL FOREST'S JOURNEY

Forest Management Controversies

1990s

Began thinning plantations for habitat objectives

High priority restoration areas identified by large-scale assessments

Roads identified to provide long-term access. Other roads waterbarred for stability.

1996-97 storm damage accelerated road decommissions and instream habitat restoration

Increased collaboration with watershed councils and other partners

Endangered Species Act - Clean Water Act

Social and Political Influences

Judicial Decisions

Endangered Species Listings

Recovery Plans & Consultation, Critical Habitats Identified

Clean Water Action Plan

Large-scale scientific assessments

Northwest Forest Plan, 1994

Reduced Budgets: $28,000,000 (1990 dollars) to $12,000,000 (2001 dollars)

Oregon Plan for Salmon & Watersheds

Partners

Watershed Councils

2000s

Forest focuses on multi-resource restoration in high priority areas on both federal and private lands.

Clean Water
Healthy Habitats
Species Recovery

SOCIAL AND CULTURAL CONSEQUENCES

The environmental legislation of the 1980s and 1990s had a profound effect on Oregon's wood products industry. New laws protecting endangered species, creating wilderness areas, repairing damaged watersheds, and limiting logging reduced the cut from federal lands, and perhaps threatened the whole industry. Through the 1980s there were about 30,000 jobs in wood products state-wide. Economists viewed these primary production jobs as support for other jobs at a 1:4 ratio, so that as many as 150,000 jobs were tied to the lumber industry in the state. About 56 percent of Oregon's timber originated on federal lands in 1988.[9]

As the 1980s ended, the economic consequences of interrupting the flow of federal timber to the mills were all too apparent in the Pacific Northwest. In October 1988, Oregon Senator Mark Hatfield and Washington Congressman Brock Adams sponsored a bill which would guarantee a federal cut of 9.6 billion board feet through the summer of 1990. The new 10-year management plans that national forests were preparing for 1990 were expected to offer long-term solutions. The Hatfield-Adams bill also sponsored research into the northern spotted owl's habitat and range. The Florence *Siuslaw News* announced that timber sales would soon resume throughout the Siuslaw National Forest, except on the Mapleton District, where sales were still restricted by a 1984 injunction. The Supreme Court later rejected the Mapleton District's request to resume sales, and then the 9th Circuit Court overturned the 1984 injunction.[10]

By 1989 the lumber industry was panicking about the timber supply from federal lands. Auction prices for Douglas fir stumpage on the Willamette National Forest reached a record of $1,567 per thousand board feet on December 27, 1989. It is

With diminishing cuts, log exports from federal lands became controversial.

questionable whether a mill could produce lumber profitably with this price for logs, but concern for timber supply had provoked a bidding war.[11]

Mills on the coast began to close in the early 1990s as the cut from the Siuslaw and the BLM's O&C lands diminished. In February of 1991, the Bohemia Lumber Company closed their mill in Drain, but continued operations in their mill in Gardiner. This historic mill town had been a center of the industry for 125 years. The Bohemia mill at Gardiner employed 300 workers and produced 700,000 board feet of lumber each day. Then, in November of 1992, Bohemia closed the Gardiner mill. The Davidson Industries mill in Mapleton closed June 3, 1993, threatening a 45-year old family business and the principal industry in Mapleton. One month later, at the end of July, 1993, the International Paper linerboard plant in Gardiner closed. This was the second large mill to close in Gardiner in nine months.

Mill closures and layoffs have always been a feature of the lumber business or any other cyclical industry. The closures of the 1990s were different, however, because they were not temporary. Mills were dismantled, the machinery sold, and the land left vacant. With the dismantling of the mills came an ominous reduction in the industrial capacity of the region.

Those who have worked in the woods and the mills like their fathers and grandfathers before them watch with uncertainty as Davidson Industries closes its doors today, signaling the end of an era of logging in the Siuslaw Valley.

***Siuslaw News*, June 30, 1993, p.1**

ECONOMIC EFFECTS

On June 30, 1993, Lane County lumber industry leader Kay King of King Logging led a demonstration protesting the proposed *Northwest Forest Plan*. King and about 200 industry representatives drove hearses carrying caskets painted with the names of timber communities. A mock funeral for the industry was held at the federal building in Portland. The Clinton Administration estimated that 6,000 jobs would be lost in the industry because of the *Northwest Forest Plan*. The industry itself estimated that 70,000 jobs would be lost. The former number reflects the number of jobs to be lost after the plan was implemented, and the latter number reflects the total number lost through the environmental legislation of the 1980s and 1990s.[12] Announcing the death of the timber-dependent communities was a little premature, however.

Steep clear-cut slope.

Projections from economists in Washington, DC, as well as the Pacific Northwest, showed that the region's economy would continue to grow despite the displacement of lumber workers. Both Oregon and Washington would create more new jobs than they would lose, thanks to the healthy economy of the 1990s. "What the forecast showed... was an expected growth in the economy despite the loss of thousands of jobs in the timber industry...But whether the people who are losing their jobs are the same as those who are finding new jobs is impossible to determine."[13] In effect, the Clinton Administration reasoned that the timber jobs could be sacrificed without harming the economy as a whole.

The bottom line [for the *Northwest Forest Plan*] on the balance is compliance with the law. One question that is not being asked and gets very little recognition is that the solution has to be in legal compliance; as if the President could have made any decision and it would have been all right, What is compliance? Being 99 percent sure it will meet the law? Being 90 percent sure? How about 70 percent, or 60 percent?

USDF Forest Service Chief Jack Ward Thomas quoted in the *Siuslaw News*, July 28, 1993

The economic changes afflicting the coast in the 1980s and 1990s are best seen as part of the nation-wide movement towards a post-industrial economy. Industrial production throughout the U.S. was diminishing during these years, as evidenced by declines in textile production, steel, machinery, and other manufactured goods. Lumber towns in Oregon were having hard times, but so were textile towns in the South and manufacturing towns in the Midwest—soon to be called "the rust belt." In the future manufactured products were to be imported but not produced in domestic mills or factories. The new post-industrial economy created jobs in services, construction, retail, information technology, and finance.

EFFECTS ON THE SIUSLAW

As the scope of the *Northwest Forest Plan* became known to the public, the Siuslaw National Forest and the Forest Service in general found itself in an awkward position. The new environmental laws required active compliance from the Forest Service and the Bureau of Land Management. These agencies were to some degree invested in the era of high timber production, however, since their budgets benefitted from timber sales. Many of the staff were from small towns on the coast and had cultural ties with the lumber industry. They also had strong ties with the region and the forest itself. It was difficult for these people to see themselves as environmental villains or political losers.

The Siuslaw's annual budget was reduced from $28,000,000 in 1990 to $12,000,000 in 2001. During the same period, the Forest's staff declined from 330 to 150. Uncertainties in budget and staffing reduced morale. In addition, the feeling persisted that the Forest Service had somehow lost prestige and the public's trust.

Where I grew up, "uncle" was a term to indicate submission. The glimpse we've all had of the President's Forest Plan for the Northwest provides ample evidence that management of federal lands is forever altered. The legal system has been used very effectively to bend our arm just about to the breaking point. It's my hope that Forest Plan serves as an overt admission that our old methods were not sustainable, that we can just say "uncle," pick ourselves up off the ground and get busy finding out if new ideas achieve what we're after.

Forest Supervisor James Furnish, 1994

The Siuslaw, like other national forests, sold surplus land and facilities as the staff declined and the Forest consolidated. The program of "Conveyances of Administrative Sites" sold the Waldport residences and the Alsea Ranger Station. Other properties including the Gardiner Ranger Station, the Mapleton residences, Big Elk campground, and the Cedar Creek administrative site are scheduled for sale. In addition to producing revenue for the Forest, these sales help the counties, since the lands sold are no longer exempt from property tax.

A lingering issue associated with the diminished cut was the Forest Service's long-standing policy of sharing timber revenues with local governments in lieu of property taxes. This practices dates back to the creation of the Forest Service. Counties could not collect taxes on federal lands, but the Forest Service compensated the counties with a share of timber sales revenue. As timber production declined, these revenues were lost, although the counties still needed to provide the same services. Oregon and Washington legislators were able to pressure the federal government to make up some of the lost revenues on a temporary basis, but no permanent solution has been found.

In the wake of the *Northwest Forest Plan*, all national forests and BLM districts in the range of the northern spotted owl saw their timber harvests cut by at least 80 percent. The Siuslaw and the Olympic National Forest in Washington had both the northern spotted owl and the marbled murrelet, so they were especially vulnerable. According to the 1996 Siuslaw *Forest Plan Merger Document*, about 8,833 acres (or 1.4 percent of the forest) remain in the Matrix lands category after lands classified as Congressionally Reserves Areas, Late Successional Reserves, Adaptive Management Areas, Riparian Reserves, and Scenic Viewsheds were defined and eliminated from consideration for logging. The 1.4 percent of Matrix land on the Siuslaw is considerably less than the 16 percent envisioned by *Northwest Forest Plan*.

The timber base provided by the Matrix lands, however, had been augmented by new management of lands in other categories. Much of the land on the Siuslaw intended for future northern spotted owl habitat is land that was logged and replanted 20 to 50 years ago. The goal for this land is to create late successional reserves of diverse species in multiple age classes. The timber plantations, however, are even-aged and consist mostly of Douglas fir. The Thinning for Diversity (TFD) program removes trees from the old plantations to lower stand density and permit introduction of species other than Douglas fir. Western red cedar, western hemlock, and Sitka spruce now contribute to the species mix on many former Douglas fir monoculture plantations. Deciduous trees also establish themselves after thinning. Since the Douglas fir removed is merchantable timber, harvests in recent years on the Siuslaw have risen to around 40 million board feet, or about 8 percent of the annual harvest during the 1960-1990 period.

Thinned stands favor diverse species. Tom Iraci photo 2008.

In addition to thinning, the Forest has pursued opportunities for reforestation and for managing plants other than trees. Special Forest Products on the Siuslaw include medicinal plants like *Digitalis*, mushrooms, greenery, and nursery stock. Tribal groups harvest native plants for traditional crafts and other purposes. New strategies for controlling invasive plants, especially in the Oregon Dunes, are having a positive effect.

THE SIUSLAW NOW: WATERSHED PROTECTION AND RESTORATION

One of the areas of emphasis in the post-1990 years on the Siuslaw has been watershed restoration. In the 1990 *Land and Resource Management Plan*, Forest managers noted that streams needed to be protected and restored for fish habitat and watershed quality. Protective measures included avoiding streams during logging, maintaining streamside vegetation, and protecting streams during road building. These measures created an ancillary problem for restoring damaged streams, however, because avoiding the streams limited access to them and made it impossible to use heavy equipment required to do the restoration work. "Building structures to create spawning and rearing habitat for fish, modifying blockages to fish passage, and providing resting pools... are often effective, but... are generally feasible only in those steams (probably less than 5 percent of the total) that are accessible to heavy equipment."[14]

Volunteer working on habitat restoration.

Before the 1990s, funds for restoring habitat were tied to timber sales. The amount of work proposed was directly related to the amount of timber harvested and the amount of damage to the watershed. Knutsen-Vanderberg funds were available for fish habitat, but these were also tied to timber sales. In effect, then, restoration of streams and riparian zones was difficult to accomplish. The total annual amount of restoration work projected in 1990 was 100 acres per year.[15]

In the post-1990 years, watershed management and restoration received new emphasis and additional funding opportunities. Watershed surveys and planning studies identified problem areas. A large portion of the critical riparian areas and salmon habitat are on private land, so watershed management required collaborative planning. Partnerships between the Forest, private land owners, and other land management agencies made it possible to do planning and implementation on a scale that could change whole watersheds. Watershed councils made up of land managers and concerned citizens created a constituency much broader than the Forest Service alone.

An excellent example of this new coordinated approach to watershed restoration is the Karnowsky Creek Restoration Project begun in 2001. Early settlers had channeled this tributary of the lower Siuslaw River to divert the stream from the bottom land, which they used for grazing cattle. Salmon reproduction zones were lost. Logging on steep hillsides had created unstable slopes. The Siuslaw Watershed Council was the lead organization for the project. The Siuslaw provided expertise and volunteers provided much of the labor. Restoration work included returning the stream to its original channel, adding woody debris to the stream, planting western red cedar and willow, removing roads, lengthening bridges, and acquiring private lands in the vicinity. At its completion in 2004, the Karnowsky Creek project won the international Theiss River Prize for conservation.[16]

Restoring the Karnowsky Creek required special equipment that would protect the fragile wetlands.

Closely related to watershed and stream rehabilitation is fisheries management. Salmon and steelhead management has been a significant issue on the coast for decades. Fish hatcheries on major streams have provided salmon and steelhead for sport and

Students participate in watershed projects.

commercial fishing since the beginning of the state hatchery program in the 1910s. In recent years, the biological community has lost confidence in the long-term efficacy of hatcheries, and embraced programs that improve the spawning and rearing habitat of native fish. Since the 1990s, cooperative management programs and partnerships with conservation groups have enabled the Siuslaw to provide professional expertise to salmon habitat work. The listing of the silver or coho salmon as an endangered species added to the importance of fish habitat restoration.

Wildlife has been another area of concern over the decades, but the emphasis has shifted in recent years from game species to endangered non-game species, including invertebrates such as the Oregon silverspot butterfly. The Grass Mountain State Game Reservation was set aside in 1913 to perpetuate elk in the central coast country. Elk habitat improvement is carried on throughout the Forest as needed.

Since the legislative programs of the 1960s, concern for the human elements in the environment has been a part of Forest planning. Laws relating to cultural resources on federal land date back the National Antiquities Act of 1906. The current mechanism for administering this law and others that protect antiquities was formulated in the National Historic Preservation Act of 1966. This legislation created the Section 106 review process that examines all Federal undertakings for potential threats to cultural resources.

In 2003 the Forest and western Oregon tribes collaborated on a heritage expedition, lower Salmon River estuary.

During the 1930s, as part of the New Deal, the federal government created programs to document American cultural resources within the built environment of structures and buildings. These programs were the Historic American Building Record and the Historic American Engineering Record, which maintain archives of reports, documents, plans, and photographs of significant structures. The major bridges on the coast highway, for example, are documented on the Historic American Engineering Record. Similar to these programs but broader in scope is the National Register of Historic Places (NRHP), created in 1966 as part of the National Historic Preservation Act. The National Register maintains reports, plans, and photos of cultural resources including archaeological sites, buildings, traditional cultural properties, and cultural landscapes. Nomination to the National Register, or a formal determination that a resource is eligible for nomination, establishes that a resource is worthy of long-term protection.

The Archaeological Resources Protection Act of 1979 gave the Forest additional legal responsibility for archaeological resources and sites. Finally, in the 1990s, amendments to the National Historic Preservation Act and the passage of the Native American Graves Protection and Repatriation Act led to closer cooperation

Tribal member shows students a tule duck decoy at the Tsalila Festival.

National Register Resources on the Siuslaw Include the Following:

Archaeological Resources –

- **Tahkenitch Landing Site (35-DO-130)**
- **Cape Perpetua Site (35-LNC-54)**
- **Good Fortune Point Site (35-LNC-55)**
- **Good Fortune Cove Site (35-LNC-56)**
- **Cape Creek Site (35-LNC-57)**

Historic Resources—

- **Heceta Head Lighthouse and Keepers' Quarters**
- **Cape Perpetua CCC West Shelter and Stone Parapet**
- **Spruce Production Railroad XII, Spur 5**

between the Forest and tribal organizations of the central coast. These include the Confederated Tribes of Siletz Indians, the Confederated Tribes of Coos, Lower Umpqua, and Siuslaw Indians, the Confederated Tribes of the Grand Ronde Community of Oregon, and the Coquille Indian Tribe. Through its Heritage program, the Forest maintains government-to-government relations with the tribal groups, particularly regarding archaeological sites, sacred places, traditional craft materials, and lifeway documentation.

In 1991, the Forest Service began the Passport in Time (PIT) program, which provided an opportunity for volunteers to get involved in cultural work, including excavating sites, documenting and restoring structures, and other hands-on efforts. The program on the Siuslaw has been popular over the years, and has contributed to our knowledge of the prehistory and history of the coast country.

Western Oregon University students and PIT volunteers excavating the Siuslaw Dunes site, 2003.

I like to look for historic sites and find some shell middens here and there, some fish weirs that no one knew about. It's kind of neat to tell [Forest Archaeologist] Phyllis [Steeves], "Hey, we've got a fish weir up on the Siuslaw. Do you know about it?" "No." So we get to take people out... Three or four years ago, I was out in the south side of the Siuslaw River, low tide, found these sticks and they were kind of interesting because they were split. Most fish weirs are just round sticks, cut sticks. These were split. And I had been out there before and never saw them before. They didn't catch my attention. Told Phyllis about it, think we went out and looked at it. Then that year they had a PIT project, we went back. Phyllis took a sample. I'm not sure what developed from that, but it was split wood instead of round sticks, which was one unusual feature. It was in an area that a lot of people go to. I talked to one of the local tribal members; he didn't know about it. "No, I didn't know there was a fish weir over there." Kind of neat to find those things.

Dave Beck Interview, 2004

THE SIUSLAW NOW: PUBLIC STEWARDSHIP

One of the most visible changes from earlier years of Forest Service management is the emphasis on cooperative decision-making. Watershed councils, public stewardship groups, and partnership with community organizations touch many aspects of day-to-day work on the Siuslaw. The new culture of the Forest Service emphasizes public participation and a pre-requisite to major policy decisions or individual projects.

Tour group on Marys Peak.

Restoration, Recreation, and Partnerships are what make this Forest tick. It's our niche, and what we do best with the natural resources we've been given on this Coastal forest. It doesn't matter whether we are assisting an off-highway vehicle rider, providing fish-friendly culverts that provide a natural path for fish to spawn in forest streams or meeting with a member of one of our valued communities we work with. Each of our tasks is unique and contributes to the whole of this Forest.

Forest Supervisor Barnie T. Gyant, 2008

NOTES

1 Siuslaw National Forest "Report on Multiple Use Management in 1962" (on file, Waldport, OR: Siuslaw NF) 1.

2 FSEEE website.

3 Bruce Gainer Interview (on file, Waldport, OR: Siuslaw NF).

4 See Gerald F. Williams, 114 to 117 for an excellent history of the controversy, 1903-1976.

5 Don Large comments, 2008.

6 Siuslaw National Forest, *Land and Resource Management Plan* (on file, Waldport, OR: Siuslaw NF, 1990) I-1. (**hereafter cited as Siuslaw National Forest *Plan***)

7 Siuslaw National Forest *Plan*, 1990, III-3.

8 USDA Forest Service and USDI Bureau of Land Management, *Record of Decision for Amendments to Forest Service and Bureau of Land Management Planning Documents Within the Range of the Northern Spotted Owl* (on file: Washington, DC, USGPO, 1994) 24.

9 *Siuslaw News*, October 18, 1989, 12B.

10 *Siuslaw News*, November 8, 1989. 1.

11 *Siuslaw News*, December 27, 1989, 1.

12 *Siuslaw News*, July 28, 1993, 1.

13 *Siuslaw News*, July 28, 1993, 1.

14 Siuslaw National Forest *Plan,* IV – 35.

15 Siuslaw National Forest *Plan*, IV – 35.

16 Siuslaw Watershed Council, "Karnowsky Creek Restoration Proposal" (on file, Eugene, OR: 1991).

APPENDIX A:

FOREST SUPERVISORS AND RANGERS

Forest Supervisors

1907	Fred E. Ames (Acting)
1907-1908	Clyde R. Seitz
1908-1913	Anson E. Cohoon
1913-1914	J. Roy Harvey (Acting)
1914-1918	Hugh B. Rankin
1918-1938	Ralph S. Shelley
1934-1935	Thomas H. Burgess (Acting)
1938-1942	Dahl J.Kirkpatrick
1942-1950	Frederick W. Furst
1950-1952	Boyd L. Rasmussen
1952-1962	Rex W. Wakefield
1962-1973	Spencer T. Moore
1973-1976	F. Dale Robertson
1976-1985	Larry A. Fellows
1985-1989	Tom L. Thompson
1990-1992	Wendy M. Herrett
1992-1999	James R. Furnish
1999-2004	Gloria Brown
2004-2007	Jose L. Linares
2007-present	Barnie T. Gyant

Spencer T. Moore (left) and Rex W. Wakefield (right) at the Smith River Ranger Station at Gardiner during winter 1962.

District Rangers

Hebo

1907-1908	George E. Leach
1908-1909	Wilbur J. Stillwell
1909-1910	George E. Leach
1910-1912	Frederick R. Russell
1912-1915	Robert J. Craig, Jr.
1915-1918	Charles T. Beach
1918-1937	Leroy E. Garwood
1937-1940	Robert Aufderheide
1940-1943	Carroll E. Brown
1943-1966	Rolfe E. Anderson
1966-1975	Wendall L. Jones
1975-1978	Joseph Astleford
1978- 1992	Ed Oram
1992-2001	Don Gonzalez
2001-present	George Buckingham

Waldport

1907-1923	Martin S. Durbin
1923-1925	Walter Sackman
1925-1930	George P. McClanahan
1930-1935	Louis H. Neff
1935-1937	Harvey A. Welty
1937-1945	Edward S. Kerby
1945-1957	Howard G. Hopkins
1957-1961	William P. Ronayne
1961-1963	Arvid C. Ellson
1963-1967	William C. Fessell
1967-1971	L. Kent Mays, Jr.
1971-1974	Robert N. Thompson
1974-1986	Robert J. Bartholomew
1986-1990	John C. Twiss
1990-1994	Conny J. Frisch
1995-2000	Doris Tai

District Rangers, *cont'd*

Florence

1907-1913	Carl H.Young
1914-1915	J. L. MacKechnie
1916-1918	George T. McCaskie
1919-1920	Edward S. Kerby
1920-1925	Purl N. Stephenson
1925-1927	Donald H. Dickerson
1927-1930	Louis H. Neff

Gardiner

1908-1911	Peter S. Rice
1911-1919	Otto Weaver
1919-1927	Donald G. Knox
1927-1931	Hobart H. Durbin

Mapleton

1920-1937	Edward S. Kerby
1937-1949	Harvey A. Welty
1949-1952	Herman C. Dill
1953-1954	Walfred J. Moisio
1954-1967	Verus W. Dahlin
1967-1973	Robert A. Perske
1973-1976	Phillip B. Wickham
1977-1987	Melvin Kessel
1988-2000	William M. Helphinstine

Smith River

1953-1957	James B. Lowrie
1957-1958	Dave F. Keiser
1958-1964	T. Carl Juhl
1964-1971	Roger L. Long
1971-1972	Richard R. Marlega

Marys Peak

1955-1957	Rex Ressler
1957-1958	Floyd J. Lyne
1958-1961	Arvid E. Ellson
1961-1963	Barrett M. Coughlan
1963-1966	John R. Skeele

Alsea

1963-1967	Ormond H. Doty
1967-1971	James C. Overbay
1971-1978	Frank Rasmussen
1978-1983	Ned Davis
1983-1987	Nancy Graybeal
1988-1997	Mike Da Luz
1997-2000	Doris Tai

Oregon Dunes National Recreation Area

1972-1973	Richard R. Marlega
1973-1975	Jerald N. Hutchins
1975-1976	Rolf D. Anderson
1976-1979	Robert L. Schrenk
1979-1986	Rick Scott
1986-1990	Conny J. Frisch
1990-1992	Ranotta K. McNair
1993-2000	Edwin J. Becker

Central Coast Ranger District

(Waldport/Alsea, Mapleton Ranger District and Oregon Dunes NRA combined initially as the South Zone)

2000-2002	Rotating District Ranger Position shared between Edwin J. Becker, Doris Tai, and William M. Helphinstine
2003-2007	William M. Helphinstine
2007-present	Pamela J. Gardner

APPENDIX B:
SIUSLAW NATIONAL FOREST TIMELINE

Siuslaw National Forest Timeline

1891
Forest Reserve System created

1905
U.S. Forest Service created

1906
Forest Homestead Act permits homesteading on Forest Reserves

1907
President Roosevelt creates Tillamook and Umpqua Forest Reserves as two of the Midnight Reserves. Hebo, Waldport, Florence, Gardiner Ranger Districts formed. Forest Reserves become National Forests.

1908
Siuslaw National Forest created from Tillamook National Forest and coastal portion of the Umpqua National Forest

1910
Extensive reforestation on the Hebo Ranger District

1914
Siuslaw staff preserves Cape Perpetua for recreation

1917
Siuslaw National Forest Land Classification Atlas completed

1917-1919
U.S. enters World War I. Army Spruce Production Division builds huge mill at Toledo, and Spruce Railroad from South Beach to Waldport

CAMP MAPLETON

1920
Dallas, Philomath and Corvallis watersheds add 2,880 acres to Siuslaw

Mapleton Ranger District formed

1921
Federal Highway Act provides funds for forest highways and roads

1925
Pacific Northwest Experimental Station established

1927-1929
Elliott State Forest created from parts of the Siuslaw National Forest and Bureau of Land Management lands. Siuslaw loses 70,000 acres

1930
Knudsen-Vandenberg Act provides funds for reforestation after timber harvest

1931
Florence Ranger District closed; Gardiner Ranger District closed

1932-1941
Nationwide Depression and the New Deal. New Deal Programs important to the Siuslaw include the Civilian Conservation Corps, National Industrial Recovery Act, Resettlement Administration, Works Progress Administration, Lumber Code of the National Recovery Administration

1933

First company of Civilian Conservation Corps arrives at Camp Cape Creek

Severe fire season, including Tillamook Burn (which does not reach the Siuslaw)

Alsea Burn

Cascade Head Experimental Forest Station established

1936

Coast highway bridges completed by Oregon Department of Transportation and WPA

Blodgett Tract Fire

Marys Peak purchases add 19,795 acres to the Siuslaw

1938

Camp Cleawox built by the CCC

1940

New Deal programs add 69,482 acres to the Siuslaw

1968

Wild and Scenic Rivers Act

1969

National Environmental Policy Act

1972

Smith River Ranger District closed

Oregon Dunes National Recreation Area established

1973

Endangered Species Act

1974

Cascade Head Scenic Research Area created

1979

Archaeological Resources Protection Act

1984

Wilderness Areas established, Drift Creek, Cummins Creek and Rock Creek

1990

Northern Spotted Owl listed as endangered

Siuslaw 10-year Land and Resource Management Plan

1991

First Passport in Time project on the Siuslaw

www.ingramcontent.com/pod-product-compliance
Lightning Source LLC
LaVergne TN
LVHW061221100826
845148LV00004B/819

* 9 7 8 0 9 1 4 0 1 9 6 0 2 *